To Roberta Bros
best wishes

Dave Clark

MW00906098

Joe's Letters

by

David W Clark

With a letter to his deceased
father from Barry Joel Clark Simpson

Bloomington, IN Milton Keynes, UK

authorHOUSE

AuthorHouse™
1663 Liberty Drive, Suite 200
Bloomington, IN 47403
www.authorhouse.com
Phone: 1-800-839-8640

AuthorHouse™ UK Ltd.
500 Avebury Boulevard
Central Milton Keynes, MK9 2BE
www.authorhouse.co.uk
Phone: 08001974150

First published by AuthorHouse 3/3/2006

ISBN: 1-4259-0027-5 (sc)

Printed in the United States of America
Bloomington, Indiana

This book is printed on acid-free paper.

Watercolour portrait: Jennifer Cline
Cover design: Barry Joel Clark Simpson

Prologue

T HIS IS a true story. All the principal characters recorded are real and lived as described. The facts of what they individually and collectively accomplished and what they individually and collectively encountered are quoted from well documented government records either here in Ottawa at the Library and Archives Canada or at the National Archives at Kew in the United Kingdom. The letters from Frank Clark to Bev Baily are completely unaltered. The facts are there to be seen, but except for what is revealed in the letters, it is the feelings and the intimate actions and thoughts of the participants that are not known — and yet they are of the greatest importance. Hence, like any other historian, I have allowed my own views to be imposed upon the events that actually happened. Forgive me if they compromise any memory or motive as it really was.

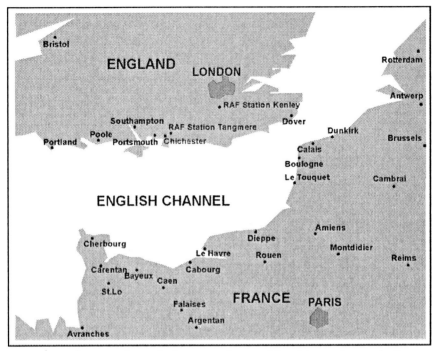

Figure 1 -- This map shows the location of most of the cities and towns in Europe mentioned in this book. Of particular interest are RAF Station Kenley near London and RAF Station Tangmere near Chichester. The base in France, centre of much of the action in the last chapters, was located close to Bayeux and the story ends halfway between Caen and Cabourg.

The following list identifies abbreviations that appear throughout the book:

2ndTAF — Second Tactical Air Force
AC2 — Aircraftsman Second Class
ALG — Advanced Landing Ground, quickly constructed air bases
ASR — Air Sea Rescue
BCATP — British Commonwealth Air Training Plan
CF Photo — Canadian Forces Photo Section
DFC — Distinguished Flying Cross
DHH — Directorate of History and Heritage (Canadian Dept of Defence)
DSO — Distinguished Service Order
EFTS — Elementary Flying Training School
EOT — end of tour (200 operations hours)
F/L — Flight Lieutenant
F/O — Flying Officer
F/S — Flight Sergeant
FW — Focke Wulf, as in FW 190 German fighter
G/C — Group Captain
GCC — Ground Control Centre
HMS — His Majesty's Ship
HQ — headquarters
Ju — Junkers, as in Ju 88 German bomber
ITS — Initial Training School
IWM — Imperial War Museum
Me — Messerschmitt, as in Me 109 German fighter
OC — officer commanding
ORB — Operations Record Book, squadron or wing diary
P/O — Pilot Officer
PRC — Personnel Reception Centre, RCAF centre in Bournemouth
RAF — Royal Air Force
RCA — Royal Canadian Artillery
RCAF — Royal Canadian Air Force
R&SU — Repair and Service Unit
S/L — Squadron Leader
SMT — Square Mesh Tracking
UK — United Kingdom, Great Britain
US 8thAF — US 8th Air Force
US 9thAF — US 9th Air Force
W/C — Wing Commander
W/O — Warrant Officer

Part One — Summer of 2004

He has outsoared the shadow of our night;
Envy and calumny and hate and pain,
And that unrest which men miscall delight,
Can touch him not and torture not again;
From the contagion of the world's slow stain
He is secure, and now can never mourn
A heart grown cold, a head grown gray in vain.

Percy Byshe Shelley — Adonais 1821

To see a World in a Grain of Sand
And a Heaven in a Wild Flower
Hold Infinity in the palm of your hand
And Eternity in an hour.
A Robin Red breast in a Cage
Puts all Heaven in a Rage.

William Blake — The Pickering Manuscript 1803

Chapter One

MAY 2004 had not been a great month in southern Quebec because the few really nice spring days that seemed to signal the start of summer and wafted spirits high were separated by spells of really cold and windy weather. On a not-so-warm but sunny afternoon, Bev Baily and Dal Russel found themselves chatting at a cocktail party at a woman's home near Knowlton, Quebec, 70 miles (112 kilometres) east-south-east of Montreal in an area known to Canadians as the Eastern Townships. These two veterans of the Second World War never met during the conflict itself, but met each other many years following the war when they both retired to country homes in the Townships. They were well into their eighties, but had been friends and neighbours for only the last 20 years.

The town of Knowlton is home to about 5,000 souls and has a fair number of elderly widows who have cocktail and dinner parties to which the many male widowers are frequently invited. For twenty-odd years Bev and Dal met each other at these events in the Knowlton area. Gradually each learned a bit more about the other's war experiences and one day in early May 2004, a few weeks before the celebration of the 60th Anniversary of the D-Day landings, a chance conversation revealed a truly astounding bond they shared.

Beverley Dane Baily ('Bev') attended McGill Officer Training Course in 1940 and joined the active force in October 1941 as a Second Lieutenant. He continued his training at Brockville and Petawawa and went overseas in May 1942. He was in the Instructional Staff of No.2 Canadian Artillery Reinforcement Unit for nine months before joining the 5th Medium Regiment of the RCA. The regiment went to Italy in November 1943 and Bev saw action as a Forward Observation Officer in the battle for the Hitler Line following Monte Casino. Rome fell to the Allied forces two days before D-Day in Normandy. A week later, Bev was returned to the UK to learn to fly small light aircraft used by artillery officers to observe and correct fire of the

3

guns. He trained over the end of the year and in early 1945 received his wings and was promoted to the rank of Captain. In fact he was engaged in a 'shoot' from which he was ordered to abort and return to base — it was 7 May 1945.

Blair Dalzell Russel ('Dal') earned his civilian pilot's license just before the war and flew out of Cartierville Airport north of Montreal. Pilots were in such demand that he was commissioned immediately upon joining the RCAF in September 1939. He accompanied 115 Squadron (renamed No.1 RCAF Squadron) overseas in May 1940 just as the Battle of Britain was about to begin. In the summer and early fall when the skies over England were filled with hundreds of darting German bombers and the con trails of swirling fighters, Dal was credited with two enemy aircraft destroyed and four shared. This action earned him the Distinguished Flying Cross (DFC). No. 1 RCAF Squadron was again renamed in early 1942 to 401 Squadron. Russel completed a tour (200 operations hours) in the UK, completed another tour leading a squadron back in Canada when the threat of invasion of the west coast by the Japanese Army seemed likely, and returned to Britain for yet another tour. He held the rank of Wing Commander (W/C) in RCAF HQ, but reverted to Squadron Leader (S/L) in 1944 to lead 442 Squadron in the Normandy Campaign under the famous RAF wing leader, Johnnie Johnson. Russel rose again to W/C before the end of the war. In the course of his career he earned the Distinguished Service Order (DSO), DFC and bar and several foreign decorations as well.

Although both men came from Montreal, they left the forces at war's end never having actually met, unless it was a chance passing on the streets of London or in the halls of some of the military support services in England. In pre-war days they might well have crossed paths many times in west-end Montreal, but there was a four-year age difference and to the young, that seems like a whole generation. After the war, each had a full working life. Bev became part of Westmount Realties soon after the war and rose to become President until it was amalgamated into the enlarging realtor A E LePage. He retired in 1982. Dal Russell had retired a year earlier. It was in this retirement period when both moved to the Eastern Townships, that they met each other as neighbours.

At the cocktail party, Bev Baily opened the conversation, "I thought you might be interested in this, Dal, because you were in Normandy. I'm in the middle of reading a book about the Normandy air war."

Dal Russel was of course immediately interested, as he led 442 RCAF Spitfire Squadron into battle on D-Day and then became Wing Commander (Flying) of 126 Wing in July in the midst of the Normandy Campaign, when George Keefer completed his tour.

Bev continued, "The name of the book is *Angels Eight — Normandy Air War Diary* written by a fellow named David Clark. That was the really curious part of it all. The book first came to my attention when I read a review of it in the Canadian Military History journal. I thought it looked interesting enough so I ordered up a copy. In the review it mentioned that a fellow whose older brother died in Normandy had written the book, but I didn't really take note of the author's name and I didn't think more of it. So it came as a complete shock to open up the book and find that David Clark dedicated the book to his brother F/L Frank Clark. My God, Dal, Frank Clark and I were in school together! He was my best friend! We corresponded regularly; I was his best man when he married; and when he and his wife June had a son, I was named the godfather!"

Now it was Dal who was shocked. "Not *the* Frank Clark — the Frank Clark whose aircraft collided with Lloyd Chadburn's aircraft a week after D-Day?"

"The very one. Why? Did you know him? Did you ever meet Frank?"

"Never knew him; never met him, but Lloyd Chadburn — hell, Chadburn was *my* best friend! My family knew his family down here in the townships from the days when Chadburn was a baby. Chad and I met and partied many times over in the UK — some of the best piss-ups of the war for me were ones in which Chad and I bent elbows together. I can't believe that Frank Clark and you were best friends!"

In this way, the two men discovered the truly remarkable fact that each had lost his best friend on the same day, in the same place in a collision that took the lives of both young men.

Theirs was an easy relationship that provided understanding without anything in the way of explanation. Bev was always affable and full of interesting thoughts and observations while Dal was a quiet fellow — one of those rare creatures who listens well. However, it was Dal who spoke first.

"Life is full of strange occurrences," Dal commented.

"That's for sure. To think that after all these years of knowing each other, we now learn about the loss of our best friends in the war. When we tell this story to other people, they won't believe it."

"This brings so many things back vividly. I can recall the young man that Chad was. I can see his face clearly. You and I survived the war while they — like so many — paid the supreme sacrifice," Dal grew pensive. "I've often wondered about how it is that some, like us, made it while others didn't. I've never been able to make any sense of it. Some say it's the good that die young, but of the thirty or more young fellows I knew personally who bought it over there, they were a pretty mixed lot — most good, but some bad and some indifferent."

Bev thought about that for a moment and then said, "There are another few coincidences that surround the story. Did you know that they both had sons?"

"No. As for Chad, I learned he had a son many years later, in the 1990s — half a century after the fact. I learned the son's name was Andrew Cockshott, and that he was born the September after Chad's death. It seems he had been adopted by a family named Cockshott — hence the name. When these facts hit the RCAF grapevine in1992, everyone I spoke to was very skeptical — especially me. Chad was a public hero; we all thought someone was trying to cash in on the celebrity. Then it was learned that this fellow was about to come over to Canada and I was asked to meet him because his father had been such a good friend with my brother and me. To be quite candid, I thought he was going to turn out to be a complete fraud. Chad was famous; Chad had a charisma about him; I thought this young man must have figured out a way to make some money out of all this. What a mistake I made! I met Andrew in 1992 when, after waiting ten minutes, he walked into the room like a ghost from the past. There he was, looking just like his father — absolutely no mistaking the resemblance. As I said, it was like seeing a ghost, a ghost who had aged very little, not as I had aged. He was Chad's son all right." Still shaking his head at the recollection, he asked, "Tell me about Frank Clark's son."

"Well, I really don't know that much about his life because we lost touch soon after the war. I was named godfather to the little fellow, but I didn't see him until I got back after the war. I visited Frank's wife, June — we'd all hung around together in high school days. She was living with her parents and Frank's son, Barry Joel. Barry was about two-and-a-half years old, a cute little fellow. And like your description of Andrew, the spitting image of his dad. I brought him a teddy bear, as I recall. But June was different, very different. As a teenager I remembered her as a very affable, outgoing, very bubbly person, but now she was much quieter, making very little fuss over the little fellow and hesitant to even mention Frank's name. She seemed a little embarrassed at my being there. Months later when I next saw her she seemed even more remote and embarrassed. She told me she was seeing a navy man named Bill Simpson and they were going to be married. I suppose she was fearful of creating a ghostly memory that might damage her new marriage. Whatever it was, the second meeting was an uncomfortable one for me and it seemed uncomfortable for June. I bade her farewell and never saw them again — neither June nor Barry."

Dal was quiet for a long while and then began to talk — in a longer monologue than Bev could remember for this normally pensive friend.

"When I met Andrew Cockshott, the whole story came out. Chad had a girl friend, Nancy MacKay — a WAAF who worked in the operations room at Hawkinge air base in Kent. Chad met her when he dropped into Hawkinge on one of his many missions. It seems three months after Chad died, Nancy MacKay gave birth to a boy she christened Ian Nicholas MacKay. I'm sure you recall the entrenched

attitudes that surrounded having a 'baby out of wedlock', as they used
to say in those days. Today it's no big deal, but then — my gosh it was
a catastrophe for any family to suffer the social indignity of having
a 'bastard' in the family. Nancy was advised not to pain Chad's
mother with the news of a bastard son, so she never tried to contact
Mrs. Chadburn — or anyone else here in Canada. She soon found
out that she couldn't work and provide for the baby too, so she had
no alternative but to put the baby up for adoption ten months after the
birth. Apparently the new adopting couple were both fine people and
re-christened the baby 'Andrew'— Andrew Cockshott. From a small
boy he had treasured a dog-eared newspaper clipping reporting the
death of W/C Lloyd Chadburn and stating that Chadburn was highly
revered in Canada. He hardly knew where the newspaper clipping
came from, but his adoptive parents told him that Lloyd Chadburn
was his real father and that a Nancy MacKay was his real mother.
As family, Andrew and his adoptive parents always bought two extra
poppies on Remembrance Day to honor Andrew's parents.[†]

"Though curious about it all through his life, it was not until
1991, at the age of 47, that Andrew told us that he tried to trace both
his birth mother and birth father. He tracked down his birth mother
in a couple of months and met with her in England. It came out in
conversation that although Nancy MacKay was advised it would be
a severe embarrassment if she tried to contact Chadburn's family,
she had followed events closely after Chad's death and collected a
spate of clippings from UK newspapers. The clippings revealed that
a squadron of Air Cadets in Oshawa and a chapter of the IODE in
Aurora — both in Ontario — bore Lloyd Chadburn's name, a lake had
been named after him, an RCAF trophy bore his name and several
streets in Oshawa bore his name as well. After the meeting with his
mother, Andrew made up his mind to go to Canada to meet all of the
interested people there — including his birth grandmother, who was
in her mid-90s. The next year Andrew came to Canada where he met
his grandmother. That was when I met him — in 1992."

---

† This information comes from Chadburn's biographer, Robert Forbes in his
book *Gone is the Angel*, Brown Books, Toronto 1997 ISBN 0-9681875-0-1.

"What a contrast — so much response to keep Chadburn's memory alive while there was so little to keep Clark's memory alive."

*   *   *

THAT was where the conversation ended, but for Bev, the revelations would continue. The book indicated that the author had a web site and Bev asked his daughter to track it down on her computer and get this fellow David Clark to telephone him. Weeks later they had the first of many long conversations and out came the story of Barry's life. Although the circumstances were unclear, it seems that June asked the Clark family to fade out of the picture so that she could raise Barry with only two sets of grandparents — her own and Bill Simpson's. Neither Frank nor June got on very well with Frank's stepmother and that probably accounts for the split. But June not only cut off relations with the Clark family, she let go all the letters Frank had written to her. Barry grew up to know the aunt who raised his father in the early years before remarriage, very little about his father in his teen and young adult years and absolutely nothing about his father as an adult or of the Clark side of the family. It was just by chance four years ago that Barry stumbled upon David Clark — his uncle from the Clark side of the family.

The more Bev thought about what Dal had told him in conversation at the cocktail party and what David said in the phone calls, the more unbelievable coincidences there seemed to be. It was in 1991 that Andrew Cockshott started to dig into the aerial collision that took the lives of Chadburn and Clark and the following year, in 1992, that he came over to Canada. David told him it was about that time when he stumbled across a reference to the collision and it caused him to plan that as soon as he retired he'd start researching it. David retired in 1993 and started researching 421 Squadron soon after. It was five years later that he had enough material to put up a web site on the topic, and of course, he had a part of the web page devoted to all the information he could glean about the Chadburn/Clark collision.[†] At that time, he found it difficult to get details, and from what details

---

† see http://www3.sympatico.ca/angels_eight/

9

he could find, it appeared there were many more questions than answers.

David told Bev that one day, out of the blue, he received an e-mail from someone who declared, "You have a photo of my father on your web site. Do you know anyone who knew him or who flew with him?"

It was Barry Joel Clark Simpson — Frank Clark's son! David replied, "Know someone? Hell I'm your uncle! I sure as hell knew him!"

Bev learned that David and Barry had been getting together frequently ever since, and had swapped all the information they could about Frank. For Barry it became a process of identifying and accepting the parts of his personality that were clearly from his father. In his high school pictures, Barry looked just like Frank did at that age. But Barry grew up aware that he was somehow very different from his stepbrother, another Andrew, and certainly his stepfather. He suspected that he was much like his father so everything he learned about Frank in the last few years became a reassuring eye opener.

Bev learned that David and Barry went over to Normandy for the 60th Anniversary of D-Day celebrations. They visited the graves of both Frank Clark and Lloyd Chadburn. It was the first time Barry had been there to see his father's grave. It was a very emotional time — moving and adding a vivid reality to the memories and the mental images. They timed the cemetery visit to coincide with a special ceremony, complete with a speech by the Governor General of Canada and other dignitaries, honouring the Canadian war dead and a great many war veterans who had come over to attend the ceremonies. Red-coated Mounties, bagpipe laments, Norman citizens representing every town the Canadians liberated and about fifty French school children made it a very special day.

They toured all through Normandy, saw the landing beaches, saw the fields that had once been the airfield where Frank took off from on the fateful day 60 years before, and they toured the many museums. They even came back thinking they had found the crash site of one of the two Spitfires!

It seems they tracked down a person who claimed to be a witness of a crashed Spitfire 'some time after D-Day' (the witness wasn't sure exactly what date) and this fellow followed up by showing them the site where it came down. The witness pointed out a hedge, about 20 feet high, that still bore the marks of some traumatic event and walked them out to the centre of a wheat field where he declared the Spitfire ended up — devoid of both wings, which were shed upon impact with the hedge. As a boy of ten, the witness jumped into the empty cockpit and pretended to fly the wrecked aircraft. In a delightful moment, this witness apologized to Barry, saying in French, "I meant no disrespect; I was just a ten-year-old boy!" Days later, the mayor of Bénouville furnished a recent aerial photograph of the vicinity and this confirmed dark discolourations in the exact spot in the field where the witness indicated the crash aircraft came to rest. They clearly found *some* crash site, but further research when they got back home virtually ruled out that it was either Frank's or Chad's.† They're still trying to figure out whose crash site it was.

In a much later telephone conversation, David told Bev, "Just to carry on with the list of parallels, coincidences and strange facts, Frank Joel Clark's father's name was Frank Allen Clark because of family ties with the Allen family of Vermont. Frank's birth mother died soon after his birth and her name was Florence.

"And how do you like this? Chad's mother's name was Florence — just like Frank's — and when Chad was only four years old, his father, Thomas Alonzo Chadburn, died and his mother married a fellow by the name of Frank Allen!"

However, Bev made the point that before anyone concluded that this whole matter was downright spooky, the three families — Chadburns, Clarks and Allens — all came to Canada just before the turn of the century from up-state Vermont where the names Frank and Florence and Joel are probably all pretty common — not to mention the Allen name.

---

† Compare the description of the aircraft above to that of the official report found on page 157 of this book.

In the very first telephone conversation Bev told David that he had a pile of letters Frank had written to him throughout the war — from joining up and going into training right through to the time of his death. These were not short letters that we have come to expect, they were 12 to 16-page letters. Bev mailed these letters to David, who transcribed them and gave the originals to Barry. That bunch of letters in his father's handwriting coming to light sixty years after the fact, was as astounding a discovery for Barry as it was for Dave. Barry read each letter thoroughly, savoured every word and finally was able to sense and appreciate, in a first hand way, the person his father was. Now Barry began to know who he really was.

Part Two — A Short Life

I saw in Louisiana a wild oak growing,
All alone stood it and the moss hung down from the branches,
Without any companion it grew there uttering joyous leaves of
dark green.
And its look, rude, unbending, lusty, made me think of myself,
But I wondered how it could utter joyous leaves standing alone
There without its friend near, for I knew I could not.
And I broke off a twig with a certain number of leaves upon it,
And twined around it a little moss,
And brought it away, and I have placed it in sight in my room.
It is not needed to remind me as of my own dear friends,
(For I believe lately I think of little else than of them),
Yet it remains to me a curious token, it makes me think of
manly love;
For all that, and though the live-oak glistens there in Louisiana
Solitary in a wide flat space
Uttering joyous leaves all its life without a friend a lover near,
I know very well I could not.

Walt Whitman —- 1860

Chapter Two

I N THE two decades that straddled the First and Second World Wars, out in the west end of Montreal, lived a thriving sector of English-speaking Quebeckers and in their midst was the red-brick, four-storey building that housed West Hill High School. Male students attended grades nine to eleven in the west wing of the school while female students attended the same grades in the east wing. The school offered courses leading to Quebec Junior Matriculation — the normal grade eleven completion of high school — and Quebec Senior Matriculation — the equivalent of and for the not-too-affluent, a substitute for, the first year of university.

In the Senior Matric graduating class of June 1939, there were twenty-seven young men and women and amongst them were seven fellows who called themselves the 'Joes'. They referred to each other as Joe Palin (alias Kerle Palin), Joe Stevens (alias William 'Bill' Stevens), Joe Smith (alias Kenneth 'Kenny' Smith), Joe Baily (alias Beverley 'Bev' Baily), Joe Wilson (alias Thomas 'Tommy' Wilson), Joe Mills (alias Ernest 'Ernie' Mills) and Joe Clark (alias Frank 'Frankie' Clark). They had known each other throughout the years of school, but it was 1938 — when they were all in grade eleven that they came together as the executive for the high school annual. Frank was the Editor[†], Bev was the Advertising Manager (and did the artwork for each section), Tommy was the Assistant Manager, Kerle was the Literary Manager and Ken was the Photography Manager. One other young man, Gerry Racine, was Art Manager. He was close to the 'Joes' but was never quite part of their group. These were the years of the 'Great Depression' when even going to a 25-cent movie

---

† The 1938 West Hill High School yearbook listed Frank's activities as, "Romeo and Juliet, Taming of the Shrew, H.M.S. Pinafore,'37 and '38, Literary and Debating Society, John Hodgson Memorial Trophy Winner '37, Rifle Club, Hi-Y, Editor-in-Chief of Annual '38."

was an extravagance so most weekend nights these young men and
their girl friends would congregate at a home that had a recreation
room in the basement. The girls brought sandwiches and the boys
provided large bottles of soft drinks. Entertainment consisted of
high school gossip, singing and dancing to music of a gramophone
or often of the boys themselves: Joe Mills on saxophone, Joe Wilson
on trumpet or Joe Baily on piano.

It was the last year of the great depression, gradually being
brought to an end by an urgent need for the Canadian economy —
indeed, the Canadian society — to wake up and prepare for war. The
economies of the Americas and of the western European countries
sank lower and lower in the 1930s after the bubble of the 1920s
ended with the frightful stock market crash of 1929. But while the
other western countries writhed, seemingly out of control, to the rock
bottom year of 1933, Germany went through a catharsis that turned
into a major economic recovery. Germany did this by supporting
the rise of an extreme right-wing party that gradually put the whole
country on a war footing. Between 1933 and 1936, Germany's Führer,
Adolph Hitler, formed an army and air force contrary to the terms of
the Versaille Treaty that ended the First World War. By borrowing
heavily from the German people, he financed an economic boom
under the stimulus of military expenditures and the building of
massive new structures and a system of new high-speed highways.
Unemployment dropped to a fraction of what it had been and run-
away hyperinflation was brought to an end. All of this came about at
the very time when the rest of the Western World's economies were
plunged ever deeper into depression.

Throughout high school the young Joes became keenly interested
in world events and in their serious conversations or in debating
sessions, spoke passionately about the absolute need for a strong
leader to lead the world's countries through Socialism or through
right-wing brute strength. The more traditional middle-of-the-road
democratic liberalism that had been the Western World's political
system for a hundred years seemed nowhere to be seen. As they came
to the end of their high schooling, several things became apparent —
Europe was moving relentlessly towards war while the United States

declared almost unanimous opposition to any European involvement, and seemed to be standing in open admiration of the miracle that Hitler had accomplished in pulling Germany up by its bootstraps.

In 1937 Adolph Hitler signed a mutual assistance pact with the Italian fascist Benito Mussolini. With the cry that Germany had to have room to expand, Hitler broke all promises he had made to foreign diplomats and began extending his borders. He annexed Austria in March 1938, occupied the Sudetenland (a part of today's Czech Republic) in September 1938, the Danzig Corridor and a part of Lithuania in early March 1939 and marched his troops into Prague to occupy all of the Czech Republic in late March 1939. Also during this period, Germany sent many new models of its military bomber and fighter aircraft to fight in Spain in support of the fascist dictator Francisco Franco in his fight to suppress the Spanish Communists in a brutal civil war. The Joes saw this war as the very epitome of worldwide political debate: extreme left against extreme right; Communism against Fascism. The modern German aircraft sent to Spain were superior to those of any other country at the time, largely because defence budgets in western nations other than Germany were languishing after the exhausting First World War. However, the German aviation technology raised a clarion call, and other nations hastened to try to catch up. Newspaper stories, illustrated with photographs of deadly Stuka dive-bombers attacking ground targets and sleek German medium bombers dropping sticks of bombs on undefended towns, rang around the world evoking widespread fear of Germany's new fighting machine. The powerful new German army and air force were proudly displayed in the broad avenues in Berlin and in the skies overhead, to a stream of diplomats and reporters who flocked to Germany to witness the pageantry of massive military parades in newly built venues that were expansive and impressive. These witnesses described in glowing terms the miracle of German economic recovery, and of Germany's territorial ambitions. Everywhere the talk turned to an impending war.

The power of the revived Germany was frightening, but the inflammatory speeches Hitler screamed at his adoring throngs and the barbarity of the repressive acts Hitler's government took against Slavic peoples, gypsies and Jews were even more terrifying. It became apparent to all — certainly to the Joes — that central Europe housed a ruthless, unpredictably dangerous military machine of, what appeared to be, unstoppable strength. The Munich Crisis and the tensions that had built up throughout the summer of 1939 caused the world to hold its breath. But although they gave in to Hitler's demands at Munich, Britain and France stated unequivocally they would go to war if Hitler attacked Poland. Hitler was convinced the other great powers in Europe were in no mood for war and so he gambled. Almost as anti-climax to this peak level of international stress throughout the summer, Germany marched into Poland on the first of September 1939 and within hours of the troops crossing the border, Great Britain and France declared war. The Canadian Government declared war on Germany 3 September 1939 — two days after Great Britain — and almost immediately, committed to provide two army divisions, Canadian naval support (largely a planned navy) and to form the British Commonwealth Air Training Plan (BCATP) — this latter was a major undertaking that would ultimately result in the training of over 130,000 aircrew members in a vast network of bases that existed only on paper.

For the Joes, 1939 was also a year of struggling for good marks, partying and trying to find work. Jobs were getting a bit more plentiful, but it would be 1940 before a plethora of new war-related jobs opened up across the land. Frank Clark managed to get hired for two weeks as a labourer repairing roads in the summer of 1938 before starting his Senior Matric and found a job at Robert Simpson's department store over Christmas of that year. Then, with the help of his father, Frank got a job as a traffic clerk with Henry Morgan department store after his graduation. He started the job in the fall of 1939 — just when the war began — and worked over the winter.

That fall and winter was a curious period from the western Allies point of view. It became known as 'the Phony War' because, after storming into a Poland split-down-the-middle between Germany and the Union of Soviet Socialist Republics (USSR) by treaty, no action was taken on the Western Front against France and Great Britain throughout the fall and into the next year. The German 'Blitzkrieg' (as it was named by Western reporters) lasted only 27 days, employed 62 divisions and 1300 modern aircraft to subdue the 40 divisions of the Polish Army. The USSR rushed troops in to occupy the eastern half of Poland whilst the Germans charged in from the west. German and Russian forces encircled and took 910,000 Polish prisoners while 100,000 others escaped through Lithuania, Hungary and Romania to fight again on the Allied side. Because of the impossible logistics of getting military forces around Germany and the USSR, Britain and France were helplessly unable to come to Poland's aid, however what they could do was bolster their defences and they rushed all available troops and aircraft forward to the borders of Germany to strengthen the forces on France's famous Maginot Line. Belgium was officially neutral so Britain and France set up a defensive line along the border of Belgium blending into the northwestern extremity of the French Maginot Line. After pulling every stop to rush battle-ready troops into place, the assemblage of nearly half-a-million soldiers sat there all winter long, waiting, waiting while nothing happened. This was the Phony War.

In April 1940, Germany quickly struck again, invading Denmark and Norway as a prelude to confronting the Allied defensive line. Hitler's offensive against the Allies was launched 10 May 1940 on a broad front 200 miles (320 kilometres) wide. His armies charged simultaneously through the Netherlands, Belgium, Luxembourg and northern France led by seven Panzer divisions deploying 1800 tanks and supported by 2500 aircraft. In three days the Blitzkrieg ran through the Dutch and Belgian front lines. Three French Armies — the First, Seventh and Ninth — together with the British Expeditionary Force drove deep into neutral Belgium to meet the invaders and stop the German advance. Although there was much armour in the German advance through the Netherlands and Belgium, the bulk of the seven mobile Panzer divisions threw out a left hook by streaming through the Ardennes to the south and raced to the sea to encircle the British Expeditionary Force and the French Seventh Army. The Dutch and Belgians surrendered 27 May and the British Expeditionary Force of some 20 divisions and half of the French Seventh Army were squeezed into a pocket on the French seacoast around Dunkirk.

At the beginning of May, the Royal Navy was asked to prepare a plan for a massive evacuation of troops. That prescient act, resulted in the assemblage of a huge flotilla of ships from small pleasure craft to every form of merchantman and naval vessel that could be found. This rabble armada succeeded, between 26 May and 4 June, to evacuate 338,000 British and French soldiers from the beaches of Dunkirk. Wading out from shore in long lines, waiting for hours in waist-deep water to be picked up by small craft, the soldiers came away with only the shirts on their backs — all their equipment and stores abandonned to the enemy. Three weeks later, France signed a humiliating surrender 25 June 1940 at Versailles — the very site of where a dispirited German Army signed the 1918 Armistice ending the First World War. Germany exacted terms upon France even more demanding and onerous than those France imposed upon Germany in 1918. A famous photograph of the time showed Adolph Hitler dancing for joy as the French generals signed the Versailles capitulation document.

In all the years that have passed since that time, it is safe to say that there has been only one period — the missile crisis of October 1962 — that created the colossal gloom that engulfed the western world, particularly Britain and the Commonwealth, as much as the events of the spring of 1940. It was a time that could only be compared with the threat to Chistiandom posed by the Turks, the threat to Eastern Europe by the Mongol horde or the threat to the Roman Empire by the barbarian neighbouring tribes. Dread and fear hung in the air. To many, western civilization seemed to hang by a thread on the verge of extinction. The USA was determined to stay out of European wars and almost all political and business leaders openly admired what Hitler was doing to stimulate the German economy. That left only Britain and France to stop the Nazis, and with France conquered and Britain's army in tatters, it looked as though the whole fabric of the 'far-flung British Empire' might disintegrate overnight. Every Canadian family sat huddled around the radio each night to hear with foreboding the terrible news that came from France. They counted the days as the evacuation of the British Expeditionary Force proceeded around-the-clock. With France defeated, Great Britain was the only obstacle to total domination of Europe by Hitler's Nazi Germany. It was an open secret that Hitler planned to cross the Channel and invade Great Britain; it was even known that he had a code name for the operation — Sea Lion. In a book entitled *'Last Ditch'* published in 1968, author David Lampe quotes German documents that define how Britain would be governed under German military law; how every recoverable stock of food, raw materials and machinery would be sent back to Germany; and how all males between the ages of 17 and 45 would be rounded up and sent to forced labour camps in mainland Europe.

The Prime Minister of Great Britain, Winston Churchill, rose before the House of Commons on the eighteenth of June. His much quoted speech said,

> "What General Weygand called the Battle of France is over. I expect that the Battle of Britain is about to begin. Upon this battle depends the survival of Christian civilization. Upon it depends our own British life and the long continuity of our institutions and our Empire. The whole fury and might of the enemy must very soon be turned upon us. Hitler knows he will have to break us in this island or lose the war."

The British Army had left most of its equipment on the shores of Dunkirk. Was there any real possibility Britain could repel an invader? As to Britain's fate, there was such a sense of gloom in the whole English-speaking world that the United States Ambassador to Britain, Joe Kennedy, declared he was convinced that Hitler would march up the Mall to Buckingham Palace within two months. It was hard to see how it could be otherwise.

To the Joes and to most young men in Canada the call was loud and clear. The world as they knew it was threatened and rapidly falling apart; there could be no course of action other than to stand up to the evil forces of Nazism and defeat them. Across the whole of the country, and as it turned out, the whole Commonwealth and parts of the United States, young men rushed to join the armed forces. The Joes were eighteen years old; they would be nineteen the next

Figure 2 — Aircraftsman Second Class Frank Joel Clark photographed shortly after enlisting in July 1940.

(family photo)

year. On 16 April 1940, Lloyd Vernon Chadburn enlisted in the RCAF in Toronto; on 14 July 1940, Frank Joel Clark enlisted in the RCAF in Montreal.

Chadburn was trained in Windsor and Uplands between April and November and received his wings and his commission as a Pilot Officer, 18 November 1940. Within ten days he was sent overseas — such was the pressure to gather as many pilots as possible to face the onslaught of the aftermath of the Battle of Britain. Many Canadians who had pilot's licenses were already in the United Kingdom — over 100 fought in the Battle of Britain, but the new trainees were just starting to be turned out. At this time, 200 pilots had already been trained in Canada and 20 of them were sent overseas. Lloyd Chadburn — 'Chad' as he was known — was one of them. He arrived too late for the official Battle of Britain but he was posted to No. 2 RCAF Squadron (later re-named 402 Squadron). It would be another year before Chad and 402 Squadron were in the thick of things.

All of the Joes enlisted except Ernie Mills and Bill Stevens, who contributed to the war effort in other ways. Ken Smith joined the navy, Bev Baily the army and Frank Clark, Tommy Wilson and Kerle Palin the air force. In the first year after joining up, several of the Joes were scattered about and didn't get to see each other. Frank was out west at Brandon, Winnipeg and Regina — all associated with basic training and Initial Training School (ITS) and Elementary Flying Training School (EFTS) — from the moment he enlisted until January 1941. He received his wings and a commission in Dunnville in March. However, in the new year the Joes managed to meet each other in twos or threes whenever their leaves permitted. Frank had two one-week leaves in March and August, each spent in Montreal. But after this period of occasional rendezvous, the Joes rarely saw each other. Kerle Palin was sent with the RCAF to Hong Kong to face the Japanese threat; Bev Baily was rotated through several artillery training centres and Ken Smith was off training for the Naval Air Arm.

*   *   *

FRANK'S training is typical of what the BCATP offered. After induction in Montreal, Frank took his first long train ride to No. 2 Manning Depot in Brandon, Manitoba. The BCATP was just being set up, and Brandon, was the second Manning Depot to open in the whole country. There Frank was housed with two thousand others in the massive agricultural exhibition building. The inductees drilled, marched, exercised, and stood guard duty. In October, he spent two weeks at No. 7 Equipment Depot in Winnipeg for more exercises

Figure 3 — The graduating class from EFTS at Windsor, Ontario. Frank is third from the left in the bottom row. Someone has recorded the casualties of this group: of the 25 graduates, eight would be killed, one missing and two made Prisoners of War.

(family collection)

and marching, before being sent back to Brandon. Four days after returning to Brandon, he was promoted to Leading Aircraftsman (LAC). Now he proudly wore the white slip of material in his cap that signified 'aircrew'. He was posted to No. 2 ITS Regina, Saskatchewan where he spent another month of drilling, together with classroom courses that dealt with the fundamentals of flight and aircraft design. He was given another medical 6 November (to determine if he was suitable for pilot training). He was posted to Elementary Flight Training School (EFTS) 27 November. Until now, all the training had been military drill designed to teach obedience and marching precision, with just a smattering of flight theory. At last, he was going up in the air; he was going to fly.

The objective of the EFTS was to get young men into the seats of a biplane aircraft and teach them to fly. The schools were civilian-operated by local flying clubs, for there was no other pool of flying expertise in the country. At the time Frank joined up, eight EFTS units were operating; when he was sent to Windsor EFTS in November, there were 16. Eventually, in early 1942, there would be 36 EFTS installations across the country. That's how quickly things were getting into gear. Students at EFTS were given classroom lectures and demonstrations, and then taken aloft in a two-seater aircraft, for their turn at the wheel under the watchful eye of an instructor. For the young inductees, the crowning moment was to 'solo'. Frank arrived at No. 7 EFTS Windsor, Ontario on 29 November 1940 — four months after the base opened. In the next two months he learned to fly the de Havilland Tiger Moth and the Fleet Finch. These sturdy little biplanes had a loose-fitting canopy covering two seats in tandem. They were easy to fly and had simple instrumentation. They served as elementary training aircraft years after the war. Frank flew with an instructor, soloed, was tested and wrote final exams. He ranked seventh in his class of twenty-five with an average of 82.9%. Graduation ceremonies were held 16 January 1941, and Frank was immediately promoted to Sergeant Pilot.

The next step was to learn to fly modern aircraft. The day after graduation from EFTS, Frank left Windsor and reported to

Figure 4 — At the end of March 1941, Frank graduated at No. 6 SFTS Dunnville, received his wings and was commissioned Pilot Officer.

(family photo)

No. 6 Service Flying Training School (SFTS) Dunnville, Ontario. At Dunnville he learned to fly North American Yale and North American Harvard monoplane aircraft — aircraft more like the fighters he would eventually fly. The Harvard had a 600 horsepower engine. It was a low-wing monoplane that sat two in tandem, in a tightly enclosed canopy. The layout of the instrument panel was similar to a front-line fighter, with a ring 'joystick' with a gun-firing button just like that of a Spitfire or Hurricane. It also had retractable landing gear, a new feature that characterized all front line fighters at the time. More important, it had some bad habits that required expert attentiveness to impending spins and stalls much like the experience of flying in combat would afford. Frank studied aircraft systems, aerodynamics, navigation, radio communication, tactics and formation flying. It was a very intense two months of training, but a period that, after allowing time to erase the heavy dread of failing, was remembered by every pilot with delight. He graduated 29 March, seventh in his class with an average of 78.5%.

At a huge ceremony at Dunnville, Frank received his wings and was commissioned to the rank of Pilot Officer. Graduation was a time for much partying and celebrating. The graduating class was broken into those who would be immediately sent overseas and those needed to train new pilots. To his considerable disappointment, Frank was selected to be an instructor. That evening Frank went on a two-

Figure 5 — Friends watch Frank beat up the airfield at Cartierville and fly some aerobatics. They are: Frank Allen Clark (Frank's father), Buddy (Frank's stepmother), Mrs. Baily (Bev's mother), Bev Baily, Ken Smith, June and an unidentified girl friend.

(Baily collection)

week leave to Montreal where he immediately teamed up with all the available Joes. After the partying and the leave was over, Frank got on a train that took him to Trenton, Ontario.

RCAF Base Trenton was built in 1929-30 and was the most modern of the RCAF's four airbases at the outset of the war. For a young man eager to fly it was an exciting place — a big, bustling facility with six huge hangars, nearly a dozen three-storey hangars, nearly a dozen three-story administration buildings, training and living buildings, and hundreds of single-engine and twin-engine aircraft dotted around the dispersal areas. Trenton was an operational air base, a training centre and No.1 Flying Instructors School — all rolled in one. Here Frank learned how to teach others to fly.

It was in May 1941 that Frank, newly qualified to train new pilots on Tiger Moths and Fleet Finches and nearly ready to teach others to fly the North American Harvard, advised the gang back in Montreal that he would fly a Harvard from Canadian Forces Base Trenton to Cartierville Airport (just north of Montreal) and fly some aerobatics. Bev Baily, Ken Smith and Frank Clark's father and stepmother — together with wives and girl friends — saw Frank fly some hair-raising aerobatics at very low altitude over Cartierville airfield. If

Figure 6 — Frank waves to his admirers after his aerial performance at Cartierville Airport.

(Baily collection)

his instructors had seen this display, Frank would have been on kitchen duty until the end of the war.

The Instructors' Course lasted six weeks. He graduated on 24 June, with a 'Cat C' rating. He was now a junior flight instructor cleared to train pilots on Fleet Finch and Tiger Moth aircraft. It took a week-and-a-half for him to receive his first assignment — instructing at No. 14 SFTS Aylmer, Ontario. But before starting the full-time job of teaching new pilots how to fly, he was given a week's leave 4 July to 11 July.

After his leave in Montreal, Frank took the train four hundred and fifty miles west, past Toronto a short distance south of London, Ontario, where he reported to No. 14 SFTS Aylmer. The base had opened only nine days before; construction was underway everywhere. In Larry Milberry's book *The Royal Canadian Air Force at War 1939 - 1945*[†], he quotes the following description of Aylmer at that time:

> "The station comprised 515 acres; with 3 pairs of parallel runways in the usual triangular layout ... W/C Norm Irwin was the commanding officer. Irwin was a well-known aviator from Whitby, Ontario, and held a pilot's license signed by Orville Wright. ... Aylmer had 40 officers, 376 men and 27 civilians on strength. ... The chief Instructor was S/L Geoff Overbury. He had 'A', 'B' and 'C' Flight Instructors in No. 1 Squadron F/Ls E.Treleaven, H.Sims and G.Hunt, and F/Ls K.Southam, A.James and Wally Quint in No. 2 Squadron."

---

†CANAV Books, Toronto, 1990

There were five double hangars and fifty other wooden buildings at Aylmer. Most buildings were completed, but the taxi aprons around all but one hangar were unfinished.

Frank began instructing, all the while studying for the next level of flight instruction qualification. On 4 December 1941, he was given yet another medical — necessary to complete the Advanced Flight Instruction Course. He graduated with a 'Cat B' designation. In this short time — July to December — the base had doubled to nearly 1100 men. There was a one-week leave 8 December to 14 December, and another 16 February to 27 February, 1942. On the first of these two leaves Frank proposed to his girl friend, Ida June Hart of Montreal. Frank and June had gone out together all through high school. They had been regulars at the parties the 'Joes' held each Friday or Saturday night. They had been in the drama club together for the hit *HMS Pinafore*, and even starred opposite each other in *Romeo and Juliet*. Now they were to start a life together. Frank was promoted to Flying Officer 30 March.

Marriage leave in Montreal began 3 April, and the next day, Frank Joel married Ida June Hart. After a short honeymoon, they moved into a rented apartment in the centre of Aylmer. This began a period that both Frank and June would regard as one of the happiest of their lives. Although he longed to go overseas where the real action was, and resented being turned down and made into an instructor, he knew that putting the war aside, he was proud of the sense of maturity and status that came through being married and he was anxious to set up a home and think seriously about raising a family. They decorated the small apartment and planned the series of guests they would invite to share their nest.

However, the business of conducting the BCATP could not wait for long and Frank resumed instructing six days later on 9 April. June became pregnant immediately, but she had no debilitating symptoms, and she didn't begin to show until late in her pregnancy. They loved the small town of Aylmer and felt exhilarated with the company of the young pupils Frank brought home with him for meals. In a letter overseas, the couple asked Bev Baily, who had been their best man at the wedding, if he would be godfather to the unborn baby. Bev happily agreed.

A week's leave was granted 17 August to 23 August and Frank and June decided to stay there in Aylmer. Frank arranged for his young eleven-year-old stepbrother to take the train from Toronto to Aylmer and stay with them a couple of days. He thrilled the young boy by taking him out to the air base and letting him sit in a Harvard. By 30 June 1942, Frank had accumulated 413 hours of flying time including 2 hours in multiengine aircraft. On many occasions Frank requested transfer overseas to get in the action, but each time he was told he was needed at home training pilots. However, by the middle of 1942 things were going better for the Allies with US Admiral Nimitz' outstanding victory over Japanese Admiral Nagumo in the Battle of Midway in May, and General Montgomery's victory over General Rommel at El Alamein in August. For the first time since the beginning of hostilities, it appeared likely that the Allies need for aircrew would diminish and the powers that be would have to start thinking about how the BCATP would be wound down. It was rumoured many of the instructors would be sent across the pond by year-end.

Meanwhile, whilst plans were considered for shutting down of the program, the actual training of pilots was at its peak. Frank was piling up flying hours. In mid-December Frank was promoted to Flight Lieutenant. This made him one of the six senior flight instructors reporting to the chief flight instructor at Aylmer. The promotion also meant even more continuous flying time, but Frank loved it. He was slated for overseas duty before Christmas but he asked if it could be delayed a short while until the baby was born. June gave birth to a son, Barry Joel Clark, on 21 January 1943 and Frank's orders were to proceed to an Operational Training Unit (OTU) and then overseas. He had logged 1200 flying hours at the time.

Frank would have preferred to go directly across the sea as soon as his notification came through because he knew all pilots would be cycled through an OTU when they got there. Instead, he was ordered to receive training on actual fighter aircraft at an OTU in Canada before going overseas. He, June and the baby left Aylmer 12

March 1943. They stopped briefly in Toronto to see Frank's father, stepmother and two stepbrothers and returned to Montreal. June and the baby moved in with June's parents where they intended to stay for the duration of the war. Frank had only a few hours in Montreal to visit with the Harts and to make a few phone calls to the Joes before boarding the train to Bagotville — the OTU in Quebec.

He arrived at No.1 OTU Bagotville, Quebec, on the thirteenth of March 1943. This was not a thing he wanted to do and he was certain there was nothing here but a waste of time. Now that he was finally heading overseas, OTU was just a transit stop — one that he didn't need.

But it turned out differently. First of all there was the camaraderie — all of his classmates turned out to have the same fervent desire to get into action that he felt. And this showed up in the intensity that the whole class exhibited when they went drinking in the small Quebecois town of Bagotville. There, the eager young English-speaking men encountered the hostility of the local French-speaking people who didn't want anything to do with this war. There had been a long-standing battle between the people of Quebec and the people of the rest of Canada over this issue of fighting a war for Great Britain. So it was that Frank was part of several ugly moments and at least two huge brawls when the whole gang of pilots teamed up to fight their way out of a bar between broken-bottle-wielding aircrew and baseball-bat-wielding 'draft dodgers'. For that is what the young Anglos considered their Franco adversaries to be — 'zoot suit' funkies who were really just draft dodgers. The people of France, who had an army equal in number to the Germans, had not fully tried to resist with conviction and caved in under the onslaught, betraying their allies by scurrying about in confusion and concentrating what power they had in places where it was of no use. In the final betrayal — their ignominious capitulation — they collaborated with the Nazis to create the neutral state of Vichy France. In the view of these young men, France had turned out to be a liability for the English-speaking world and now this part of Canada was turning out to be the same. This constant friction added spice to the stay at Bagotville and when he left, Frank could honestly say that he had enjoyed the conflict as much as the vital information he learned while there.

Figure 7 — Frank and June with baby Barry taken while Frank was on embarkation leave, May 1943.

(family collection)

In the course itself, Frank learned to fly Hawker Hurricane Mark II fighter aircraft of the type used in the Battle of Britain. Although now superceded, these aircraft were front line, with lots of power, high speed, high rate of climb and superb flight characteristics. They sported eight machine guns in the wings. The pilots were taught battle formation flying, armament, gunnery practice on aerial targets and ground targets and battle tactics. In addition, they attended lectures from veterans who told them what it was really like to be in combat. Experienced fighter pilots, back in Canada after completing a tour of duty, supplemented the instruction team at OTUs. F/L Wally McLeod was one of these. He was posted to Bagotville in March 1943 after a very successful tour in Malta. McLeod had 13 victories to his credit at that time; he was a passionate fighter pilot who strove to pile up a heap of victories greater than any other Canadian. At his death in late 1944, McLeod's total was 21 enemy aircraft destroyed. That made him the highest scoring RCAF fighter pilot. (Buzz Beurling was the highest scoring Canadian, for he is credited with 31½ victories, but he scored all but one of these while serving in the RAF.)

Frank left Bagotville 16 May 1943 and headed home to Montreal for two weeks pre-embarkation leave. He stayed with June and the baby at June's parents.

On the nineteenth of May Frank sent this wire to his friend Bev Baily who was in England:

"19 MAY 1943

2NLT LIEUT BAILY B D
5TH CDN MEDIUM BATTY RCA
CANRECORDS LONDON

HAPPY BIRTHDAY ON MY WAY AT LAST

JUNE FRANK BARRY CLARK"

Ten days later, his family and in-laws saw Frank off on a train to Halifax from the old Bonaventure Station in Montreal. It was the last time any member of the family saw him again. The next day, after an all-night ride through the Gaspé and into the Maritimes, Frank reported to the embarkation depot at Halifax, Nova Scotia. He was assigned to RCAF No. 14 Transportation Pool in Halifax. Now came a frustrating period. For two weeks he cooled his heels with thousands of soldiers, sailors and airmen coming and going through the busy port of Halifax.

Chapter Three

I T WAS the sixteenth of June before Frank sailed on HMS Louis Pasteur, crowded on the ship with a couple of thousand other troops. The accommodations and food were excellent — although always enjoyed in crowded conditions — and Frank was delighted with the trip. Frank had never stayed in a large hotel or a ship and so had never known such luxury and preferred treatment. The eight-day crossing was uneventful under mostly cloudy skies, reasonably calm seas and most important of all — no encounter with U-boats. Upon arrival in England, he reported to No. 3 RCAF Personnel Reception Centre (PRC) in Bournemouth, on the Dorset coast. This south coast town was located just west of Southampton and had been a favourite resort town for over a century. But in the Second World War it was almost completely taken over by Canadians in the RCAF — a place where everyone met their many friends as they passed through to other assignments. The seafront was lined with resort hotels converted to housing for the airmen while the beach in front bristled with barbed wire and landing obstacles. Here and there were the small square pillboxes erected right after Dunkirk when Britain expected to be invaded at any moment. Within hours of arriving at No 3 PRC, Frank tried to contact his friends. In a telegram to Bev Baily, he wrote enthusiastically:

"26 JUNE 1943

POST OFFICE TELEGRAM

HERE I AM OLD BOY STOP CAN YOU CONTACT ME AT HIGHCLIFFE HOTEL BOURNEMOUTH AS SOON AS POSSIBLE LOVE AND KISSES FRANKIE"

His orders were to report in every day to an administrative officer — nothing more. For ten days he did nothing but attend orientation courses, wander around discovering Bournemouth, watch a few movies, meet dozens of other airmen he had trained with and wait for assignment to an operational squadron. By phone Frank contacted three of his school friends — Bev Bailey, Ken Smith and Tommy Wilson. In a bevy of phone calls and telegrams they immediately made arrangements for the four 'Joes' to meet in London. Frank was granted leave starting the third of July — the agreed upon meeting date.

For two days, from dawn to well past midnight, they had a grand time in London. All the private clubs opened their doors to officers and often generously showered their guests with drinks. In addition, there were many reception centres like Canada House that welcomed the thousands of Allied soldiers, sailors and airmen as they passed

Figure 8 — Four of the 'Joes' met in London in July 1943. Lt. Ken Smith (Naval Air Arm), Lt. Bev Baily (Royal Canadian Artillery), P/O Tommy Wilson and F/L Frank Clark (Royal Canadian Air Force).

(Baily collection)

though, providing snacks and often organized dances or other social events where young men and young women could meet. On the third day, Ken Smith's 48-hour pass ran out and he had to return to base. The other three 'Joes' — Frank, Bev and Tommy — travelled by train to Edinburgh where they continued their partying, their round-the-clock discoursing and sightseeing. In the endless chatter between them, Tommy described flying Spitfires in OTU and complained how long it was taking to get a posting to an operational squadron. Frank was dying to fly a Spitfire and eagerly soaked up Tommy's description. They all conjectured as to what would happen next in their military careers. Bev felt certain he'd be sent to the Mediterranean theatre while both Tommy and Frank claimed to have heard rumours that pilots about to be posted to operational squadrons were being sent there as well, and they speculated about when they would all go on leave together in Cairo. One of the other considerations both Tommy and Frank anguished about was how likely it was that they may be re-mustered into Bomber Command because loss rates were so high that bomber pilots were greatly in demand. The partying was fast and furious and the week flew by quickly. Before heading south from Scotland, Bev and Frank accompanied Tommy back to his OTU at Grangemouth a few miles west of Edinburgh. When it was over,

Figure 9 — The two best friends, F/L Frank Clark and Lt. Bev Baily on a street in Edinburgh.

(Baily collection)

they all agreed it was the best leave it could be — a once-in-a-lifetime experience.

A week later Frank managed to get up to London to meet Ken Smith again — both were on a 48-hour pass. He wrote a long letter to Bev describing his life at Bournemouth:

"F/L F J Clark
RCAF England
24 July 1943

Dear old Joe,

Got my welcome letter this morning and am replying at once. I was waiting to hear from you before writing, as your future was somewhat uncertain when I left you at London and I didn't want to have this letter following you all over England until I was more or less sure where you would be. I rather thought, as a matter of fact, that you might have been shipped off to Sicily or North Africa when they disclosed that Canadians were in on that show.

Glad you found your kit OK and were able to get definite instructions as to what you were to do. It was good to hear that you enjoyed your leave because, for myself, I haven't had such a wizard time since Newboro. Don't need to tell you how swell it was seeing you and Tommy again as my letters from Canada, I think, gave you a good idea how much I was looking forward to the meeting — and by gosh the real thing was very far from being a disappointment. My old theory that expectation is greater than realization proved itself wrong most definitely in this case. I wrote Junie a 16-page letter telling her all about it — something which I haven't done since my wooing days. And even then I think the longest epistle she ever had from me was 12 pages of mush. She got my cable, which I sent from London and from her latest letter appeared almost as excited over the whole affair as I was.

I took off a couple of days last weekend and met Kenny in London. We had a short but enjoyable get together — which means I have seen all the Joes within a month almost. It took some buzzing around though — Joe Mills and Joe Stevens in Montreal, Joe Baily and Joe Wilson in Scotland and Joe Smith in London.

Since I've come back from leave I have also seen Gerry Racine and Bob Vincent who are staying here. Gerry just arrived in England and Bob has finished OTU and is on leave waiting posting. Just a few minutes ago I met F/L Lunan — remember him at West Hill? He used to teach ninth year — he and Dudley Wilson were the best-dressed men at dear old alma mater. He also has just arrived over here.

By the by — I also left something (slippers) at our lodging place in Edinburgh so wrote to Miss Frost about them and have just received them back plus your pajamas. So I think I'll mail you your pajamas using your old address and they should eventually catch up with you. The reason I want to send them off now instead of keeping them till we get together again is because I'm rather expecting to be posted soon. So if you write me before you hear from me again, leave the No.3 PRC off my address and use the address at the top of this letter. It will get me at my new address then without coming all the way down here. In any case, should I be posted, I'll write you immediately giving my new address if possible. Wherever and whenever I do go,

I'll be there for the better part of two months I imagine, so you won't have to worry about chasing me around at various stations.

Well, old salt, I bloody well hope we can get together again soon. Keep me posted and I'll do the same for you. Ta ta for noo.

Frankie"

Frank spent over a month in Bournemouth, meeting countless fellow Canadians, encountering old friends, joining several drinking clubs and reporting in once a day to his superior officer. But he hadn't flown since Bagotville and he longed to get in an airplane and fly — he missed it terribly. Days of disappointment were spent waiting for a posting, hoping it would be directly to an operational squadron. All the while he wandered about and found that nothing seemed to be happening, for him or for many others with whom he shared the boredom. Spending two weeks in Halifax doing nothing was bad enough, but here in Bournemouth Frank waited a whole month. Then when orders came through, it was not a posting to an operational squadron as he wished, but rather he was posted to another OTU. This was not good news, but at least he would be flying again. Immediately he wrote his best friend, Bev, giving the new address:

"Saturday 31 July

Dear old Joe,

Just a few lines in haste to let you know that I am being posted from here sometime next week to an OTU. My new address will be;

F/L F J Clark J.4924
RAF Station
Kirton-in-Lindsey
England

Expect I shall be there for a couple of months so you can use that as a permanent address until I advise you of any further change.

Doubt I'll be able to get any leave now until I finish the course there, but might be able to sneak off on the odd weekend. In any case, I'll write you from there when I find out the gen on such things as leave.

You can't imagine how pleased I am at the prospects of flying again. I was really getting browned off at this place.

I got a couple of days off at the beginning of this week and whipped up to see the Colonel Lent for whom I've been carrying around a bottle of scotch from Aunt Doris since leaving Canada. Had an absolutely wonderful time in the Army and think now that the 'boys in brown' aren't such a bad lot after all — with one or two exceptions of course. Don't know if you remember Ross Lent (the colonel's son) or not, but he's a 1st Lieutenant now and we drove down to see him and had a great old drink at his Mess. He is in a Company Mess, which I imagine, is about the same size as yours (as regards numbers I mean) so we had a grand cozy little evening and drank up all the goddam scotch. I felt rather bad about that when I left, but after stops at the Colonel's favourite pubs on the way back to his station, I got to feel quite happy about the whole thing.

By the way, while at the Colonel's station (No. 1 NETD) I met young Kenny Carstairs who is on his way back to Canada to take an OCTU course. Said he had spent his last weekend with Hal. Also met several old cronies from Brampton who are in the Lorne Scots.

How are the courses going? Don't know how I'm going to take to this working business again after a 5-week holiday.

Haven't heard from old Joe Wilson since we saw him on leave. Talked to Kenny on the phone a week ago Thursday but nothing in writing yet. The letters continue to pour in from Junie — Barry has two teeth now and has a job selling papers on the corner of Girouard and Sherbrooke, Junie is contemplating taking a morning job at McGill (as a steno) sometime in August and work from 9 to 1, to keep me out of the poor house over here, your Mom and Dad are on holidays I think but you probably know more about that than I do, Stan Jackson is back in Canada (P/O — RCAF) to take his training for a pilot, Shirley Jackson (Guy Newson's old flame) is going to have a baby and I'm well, how are you?

Hope we can get together again Joe and soon — I want to hear 'Stardust' and 'Moonbeams are sent from heaven' — sigh!

Success to Temperance
Frankie"

The continuing rivalries between army, navy and air force were a source of considerable ribbing for the 'Joes'. Air force personnel used to distinguish airmen (blue jobs or boys in blue) from army personnel (brown jobs or boys in brown). At any point in a conversation Bev and Frank threw in this good-natured joshing.

*   *   *

O N THE second of August, Frank reported to No. 53 OTU at Kirton-in-Lindsey in Lincolnshire, about 100 miles (160 kilometres) north of London. Here he put in the first flying hours he experienced since leaving Canada two months earlier. The aircraft he flew at OTU was the Supermarine Spitfire Mark II. Frank was thrilled, for these models were hotter aircraft than the Hurricanes he flew in Canada. For a young pilot, getting into a Spitfire for the first time was like making it to the National Hockey League and skating with the Montreal Canadiens. The power, the responsiveness, the enormous ability to climb, roll, dive, turn tightly and swing around the sky were just an ecstasy for anyone who loved flying. And when well trimmed, the Spitfire nearly flew itself — such was its responsiveness. Frank worked hard at the OTU, even though it was a repeat of what he had been taught at Bagotville. He only found time to write to his friend Bev three weeks after arriving at his new base. In the letter he has begun to feel much more at home in England and can comment candidly about English women:

"RAF Station

Kirton-in-Lindsey
Saturday 21 August 1943

Dear old Joe,

Have just tucked away a tidy tea, so feel as much in a writing mood as I ever will I suppose. Gone are the days when I used to be happy in wandering about with a pencil in one hand and a piece of blank paper (which usually remained blank) in the other saying, "God, I must write a book!" Now I just wander about with empty hands and a blank mind thinking, "Goddamit, I'm away behind in my correspondence." Luckily though, for my own good name, I get a great stack of mail every so often which has the effect of rousing in me a great self-shame at my lethargic 'correspondentivity' and stirring me to great deeds — then I usually sit down and write a bloody letter to some unfortunate soul. Same happened yesterday, but as I went on a serious little pub-crawling expedition last night, couldn't settle down to do my bit till today. So — how the hell are you, Joe?

The mail service is a little confusing in this country. Yesterday, I received a letter from you dated 8 August. Today I received another dated 19 August. However I certainly am bloody glad to hear from you and know that you are still in this country even if quite a distance from where I am. For some reason or other I've been rather expecting you to pop off to Sicily these last few weeks. But so far so good. You have probably now consulted your maps and pinpointed my position — but if not am in the county of Lincolnshire and rather near Lincoln. That, of course, is quite a general estimation.

You apparently enjoyed your course in Wales, but I'm just a little doubtful, after reading your first letter again, if all those 40 pages of notes deal solely with the technique of mine-lifting. I imagine you were lifting <u>land</u> mines, so to speak, and am curious to know what kind of technique you used to pick up at 2 am <u>in the water</u>. Rhyl sounds 'rhyly' all right and add my vote that we head thereto on our next leave.

Speaking of which reminds me that I expect to finish here about 21 September or thereabouts — maybe a few days before or after. And after finishing here I will be eligible for indefinite leave until I am posted to a squadron. And that indefinite leave will be at least a week and more probably two or three. So it looks as if my leave should pretty well coincide with all or part of yours. In which case Rhyl is going to take an awful beating. There is something stirring in my blood these days, Joe, and it's not old age. Being a married man I rather blush to mention it, but on the other hand, being myself I must confess that Rhyl (as per your description of its abundance of sweet young things) sounds quite intriguing.

Now for just a moment to bring you up to date on the movements of yours truly since I last wrote you. I left Bournemouth on the third and arrived here the same day after alas spending half the trip in the ruddy baggage car — and that after a strenuous farewell party the night before. However my luggage at least, arrived here in good shape. It's a bloody wizard station this — built on and in peace time style and is very comfortable with all sorts of sports facilities, billiard tables, fairly good food and nice bar. Best of all really good bat<u>men</u> for a change.

I'm flying exactly the same type of aircraft that Tommy flew and doing exactly the same course — so all our drunken argument in Edinburgh's parks was for naught. I imagine I'll end up doing the same thing as Tommy, but that of course is in the future and therefore subject to infinite and incomprehensible change. All that other business I told you about fell through for our bunch. I'm just as happy though as I've always wanted to fly this type of aircraft. I've had several hours in 'em now and so have seen a fair amount of England from the air — bloody confusing.

Am really leading the life of Reilly here as the course is exactly the same as the one I had in Canada and therefore requires a minimum amount of work. As a matter of fact, the few of us here that had an OTU in Canada have had our course here cut short by a couple of weeks which means getting to a squadron and maybe some action a lot sooner. All of which makes me quite happy.

There are three or four good pubs in the immediate locality and a little further afield, a town called Scunthorpe which offers various forms of entertainment. Am gradually settling down to a rather pleasant existence in this country and have been circulating a bit more freely with the gentle sex since I last saw you. I find them amazingly frank and friendly. They apparently all seem thoroughly familiar with the facts of life — a situation which falls right in place with the wartime slogan 'let's not waste time.' All in all Joe, I'm looking forward with even greater anticipation to our next leave than I did to our first. I feel I know my way around a bit more now than I did then. Am saving up pennies so it can be a bang-up time.

The news from home you probably have as recent as mine, so won't say much in that line.

Had a letter from Kenny the other day which didn't say much but that he had heard from Tommy while on leave and in main answering the note I dropped him about my posting.

Alas a letter from Doris and the Brampton folks send their best regards to you — Doris said that there is a parcel on the way for me with a nice drop o' Canadian rye enclosed. Hope it arrives in time for my leave.

Junie's letters were full of joy as she finally received a great stack of letters from me. For a month or so all she was getting were my cables and she consequently thought I was sort of shirking and all that sort of stuff. So she is happy now having received tangible proof of my continued devotion. Her bike trip with Cyn Tindall and Ben Wilson was quite a success. They covered about 105 miles. I sent her copies of the pictures we took while on leave and she has shown them all round including Mary who has been spending some time in Montreal apparently.

Glad to hear you received a copy of the West Hill High School Annual. I have not as yet. Would certainly appreciate seeing yours.

About Gerry Racine and your razor — I know he brought one over for you as he told me that in Bournemouth and I gave him your address. But he left Bournemouth a few days before I did and I'm not sure just where he is now. You could contact him though by writing to No.3 PRC. He is an F/O by the way — don't know his number.

Better write 'finis' to this as it is dinnertime and I must shave and tidy up first. Don't strain yourself trying to answer this Joe — but do let me know when you get some time off and have nothing else planned as I might just be able to wrangle a 48 too. Will let you know more definitely about my leave when I know myself, and if we can get together for a week or so suggest we plan in advance a bang-up time for ourselves — it may be our last for quite some time if I do get my posting to the Middle East.

Thanks for the letters and ta ta for noo,
Frankie"

The sounds of home and hearth seep through this letter but Frank, far from home and liberated a bit by that distance, comments on the openness of English women. If these deep urges amounted to anything we don't know, but he clearly acquiesces to the responsibilities of being a young married man who has just recently welcomed a young son into the world.

Still another leave came along — this time for two weeks upon completing the OTU course of instruction. Immediately, he tried to drum up support from the 'Joes', but unfortunately, he wasn't able to get together with any of them, so he elected to take a general course up in Oxford that dealt with the broader issues of the war and with its aftermath. Frank travelled to Oxford, enjoyed that beautiful city and found the course, and the attendees, to be most interesting. Once more he returned to Bournemouth and wrote a letter to Bev:

"No 3 PRC
Bournemouth, Hants
1 October 1943

Dear old Joe,

Well, where the hell are you now? I phoned you the other night, last Saturday to be exact, and was told that you wouldn't be available for a week. So figure you must be out on a course or something.

Had a fairly good time up at Oxford. The course was quite interesting because it was so general. There were about 60 on the course — about an equal number of English, American and Canadians. There was everything there from an AC2 and American Red Cross gals to a brigadier general and a flock of majors and colonels. Oxford is really a beautiful place and a trip there just to see the place would be worthwhile in itself. Left there last Friday, spent the night in London and reported in here at Bournemouth one day late and flat broke.

Had a cable from Junie the other day telling me that Kerle has officially been reported prisoner of war in Japan. The Palins of course are overjoyed to know that at least he is alive and well. I certainly don't envy the poor son of a gun though. But in any case the Joes are still all alive and kicking which I hope will still be the case on the final Armistice Day.

Am enclosing some of the pictures we took at Edinburgh. Keep them if you want them as I had them made for you. Will send you the London pictures as soon as I have some more printed.

Haven't had much mail from home for the last three weeks so can't give you much news. Jeannie had a birthday party for Ernie and Junie was there — I think from what she said in her letter that the cable we laboured over so hard in London arrived that day. Did we remember to wish old Joe 'Happy Birthday' in the final version we eventually dispatched? If so, it arrived very opportunely.

Had a parcel from Doris in Brampton the other day which included a bottle of Seagram's 83 rye whiskey. What about getting a weekend and coming down to see me — have just written to Tommy asking him to do the same. Think I might be able to fix you up with bed and meals and could in any case show you around the drinking part of the town in style as I have joined no less than three private drinking clubs in the last week. So what about trying to get down here for a couple of days sometime soon. Drop me a line if you figure you could make it.

Gerry Racine is down here right now and I told him once again of your plight. So he said he would try to get in touch with you as he has an extra razor which he could let you have if the one he sent you hasn't shown up yet.

All the boys I was with at Kirton are down here too. We have absolutely nothing to do. Once a day I have to report to some Squadron Leader — any time at all during the day just whenever the spirit moves me and that is my work for the day. We've been operating almost entirely by night since coming down here and have been using the daylight hours for sleeping and general resting up purposes. Wonderful war this — might just as well re-muster to the bloody Boy Scouts.

Have had a couple of letters from Tommy since our do in London. You probably have too as he mentioned writing to the Joes. He got his promotion to F/O which I am very glad to see. He has moved, by the way, up to Digby Lincoln, but is still in the same squadron.

Had a letter from Jeannie Douglas the other day. Didn't have much news in it as it was dated 14 August. Spent most of its time following me around England. Only news from my family is that the young son has seven teeth now. Guess it won't be long now before I start paying dentist bills.

We're just about to be hit here by a great thundering rainstorm — so if you see a few drops and smears on this letter you'll have to excuse 'em as we smashed one of the windows in our room the other night and it has left us pretty well open to the elements.

Well can't think of much else to say except that I hope you'll be able to arrange a couple of days leave down here at Bournemouth. If not though, what about my coming up to bother you. Be seeing you soon I hope.

Success to Temperance
Frankie"

The reference to Kerle Palin in Frank's letter records a sad fact. Of all the 'Joes', only Kerle saw action almost immediately after joining up, and it was action of the worst possible type. He proceeded through flying training quickly and was immediately posted overseas in the Pacific Theatre. The RCAF personnel sent to Hong Kong had nothing in the way of modern equipment and in great desperation, flew Tiger Moths with machine guns strapped to the top wing against the Japanese Zero fighters — less than a child David against a greater-than-life Goliath. This noble but futile effort was over before it began. When all had been lost, Kerle escaped with his confreres to Singapore and thence to Java (modern day Sumatra). His parents were advised that he was reported missing. Apparently Kerle and a number of other airmen went into the hills in Java, hiding with guerillas. Unfortunately he was captured and suffered the indignities of spending the rest of the war in Japanese prisoner-of-war camps. But he survived. When the war was ended and he was released, he wanted to return to Canada get a medical degree and go back to Java to become a physician. Unfortunately his grades at McGill University were not high enough and he re-directed his career into hospital administration where he flourished for many years in a large Toronto hospital.

*　　*　　*

BACK cooling his heels in Bournemouth, Frank was once again doing nothing except checking into the HQ to prove he was still alive and then whiling away the day until he could visit his drinking clubs after five. He often walked down by the shore and this usually gave him time to think. On one very warm July day in mid-morning, he found himself sitting on a bench under a tree looking over the tangle of barbed wire out at the Channel. Over the hills behind him the sky was a watery blue but it shaded into the light grey of the mist that hung over the sea and blended sky into water — all this light grey colour. The tide was going out and the sea was calm with only a long swell of waves mysteriously appearing in the fog, rolling in lazily and collapsing over the pebble beach. The scene reminded him of his days at cottages in summers gone by, but more recently, it was much like the scene that he and June sat mesmerized by last summer. June was in her early months of pregnancy and Frank had a 48-hour leave. He signed for a jeep at the base and the two of them drove to the shore of Lake Erie where they had a picnic at a spot just like this — except for the barbed wire!

As he strained to see through the mist his eyes detected a stain in the middle of the haze that with time, emerged as a hazy horizon.

The sun was burning off the mist and soon, with the horizon far more evident, bright flashes shone through the haze. Minutes later the flashing reflections of the sun were like a swarm of a million fireflies blinking. Was this what flak centres will look like from a distance? He thought it would and his mind immediately jumped to the question of fear. All those who had been in operational combat said that the fear never leaves one. At times it could be drowned out by good company and beer, but in the night and early hours before a mission the taste of fear crept into every pilot's mouth. It was metallic and dry. Frank remembered the feeling of butterflies in his stomach before going on stage with the drama club, but somehow he knew this would be worse. Experienced pilots said they learned to live with fear but the real test occurred the first time someone fired at you. The immediate panic that one experienced could completely immobilize one for a moment and then the urge to run was overpowering. If one could gather one's senses and charge into battle, the test was passed. How would he fare? Could he overcome the urge to flee? He wondered.

*   *   *

O N THE third of August Frank was ordered to go to an OTU — this time it was the OTU at Grangemouth up in Scotland on the Firth of Forth. This was the OTU where Tommy Wilson had been training just before the London and Edinburgh rendezvous. It was the one he and Bev visited when they accompanied Tommy back to his base.

Going to a second OTU course was most disconcerting, but Frank set off once more. However, he no sooner arrived in Grangemouth when new orders caught up with him and posted him to an operational squadron. In absolute delight, he immediately turned around and took the train to join RCAF 421 'Red Indian' Squadron stationed at RAF Station Kenley, a little south of London. It was a gift from heaven! His long-awaited dream was coming true! It had taken four months from the moment he arrived in England, and over seven months since he was ordered to go overseas, but now he was finally going to fly with an honest-to-god operational fighting unit.

Chapter Four

THE NEXT day, the thirtieth of October, Frank reported for duty to RCAF 421 'Red Indian' Squadron operating out of RAF Station Kenley. Just 14 miles (22 kilometres) due south from the centre of London, still in the London suburbs, are the towns of Chaldon, Caterham, Worlingham, and Kenley. The city of London lies in a basin surrounded by rising ground to the south and north. To the south, the land rises to a plateau and escarpment that is part of the North Downs. Today the M25 highway runs at the base of this

Figure 10 — The Officer's Mess at RAF Station Kenley as it looks today. It is now occupied by offices of the UK government and the airbase is used as an amateur glider park and dog-walk.

(author's collection)

escarpment. Cutting north-and-south through the raised ground of the escarpment are several valleys. Frank got off the train at Whyteleafe Station on the outskirts of the town of Kenley in one of these valleys. He threw his dufflebag over his shoulder, grabbed his handbag and trudged up the long sloping road to the main entrance and into the Officer's Mess. The airbase sat on tableland about 100 feet above the valley floor and the rail-road station. It was an exciting, bustling day fighter airbase — exciting to see, and exciting to sense the energy and vibrancy of the place. Frank felt enormously proud to finally be in the role he had been preparing himself for the last three years. But in looking around he realized there was so much more to learn.

421 RCAF Squadron, together with 403 RCAF 'Wolf' Squadron, had been known as the 'Kenley Wing' but was just recently designated 127 Airfield, 17 Fighter Sector, 83 Group, Second Tactical Air Force (2ndTAF). The Allies were preparing to invade Hitler's 'Fortress Europe' in the months ahead, and in order to ensure air superiority over the beachheads and to support the British and Canadian ground forces as they marched across Europe, parts of Bomber Command and Fighter Command were assembled to form the Second Tactical Air Force (2ndTAF). Support for the American ground forces in Northwest Europe was to be afforded by the newly-formed U.S. Ninth Tactical Air Force (US 9thAF).

Patterned after the very successful Desert Air Force that substantially helped Montgomery's victory in Africa, each tactical air force consisted of numerous medium bomber, fighter-bomber, fighter, and reconnaissance wings intended to work in close support with the army. Although the bomber elements with their longer range, could continuously offer support flying from English bases, squadrons of fighter, fighter-bomber and reconnaissance aircraft, with their short range, could not. Air time from England to the coast of Normandy (the planned target for the invasion) was one-half hour for the Spitfire. Even with extra fuel tanks, the Spitfire had a maximum endurance of slightly over two hours — not enough to get to the border of Germany and back. It could not escort the heavy bombers further. The solution was simple — for the invasion of Europe, the support aircraft would have to move forward behind the army as the Allies advanced to Germany, moving from base to base as necessary. This meant building new advanced air bases close to the front and quickly moving into them. Pilots and ground crews had to learn how, on short notice, to pack half of everything into trucks and move, set up immediately and operate from a new field while the other half of the equipment caught up the following day.

Spitfire squadrons first learned how to do this in the summer of 1943. Until this time, RAF squadrons and those of the Commonwealth who patterned their activities after them, were autonomous units with their own control, maintenance, medical and kitchen staff. For instance, before the necessary reorganization of squadrons, 421 Squadron had 25 to 30 pilots, four administrative officers and about 120 airmen ground crew. These autonomous squadrons moved from one base to another often taking over the equipment of the squadron they were replacing. The actual move consisted of loading everyone on a train and sending them to the new base. The bases where they were going were completely equipped with kitchens, sick bays, repair facilities, spare parts inventories, radar control facilities — all the necessary workings of an air base. Moved around as they required rest or rebuilding, or thrown into battle as reserves dried up, this is how the autonomous squadrons operated in the First World War and how they operated until 1943. They were invariably grouped with one or two other squadrons and the assemblage took the name of the base from which they operated, being referred to as the Martlesham Wing or the Digby Wing, or in this case, the Kenley Wing.

But the need to completely dismantle a base, move it a hundred miles and reassemble it meant there would have to be much more integration of function. The solution was to modify the structure so that individual squadrons would have only three or four personnel other than the pilots themselves, while a central headquarters organization housed all the other complex functions. A squadron like 421 Squadron would now have 25 or more pilots, an adjutant, a medical officer, an intelligence officer and a couple of clerical personnel — and that was all. Medical facilities, kitchen facilities, servicing and maintenance, repair and overhaul, radar control and other support functions would be provided by a pool of airmen from the wing headquarters. The wing not only absorbed all the infrastructure personnel from the squadrons, but also received over 100 drivers and 200 trucks to effect the transfers. They also received many hundreds of tents. Thus when Frank joined 127 Wing at the end of October 1943, there were 33 officers and airmen in 403 Squadron, 36 in 421 Squadron and 590 in 127 Wing HQ — a total of 659. When 416 Squadron joined the wing in April 1944, the total rose to 850 personnel.

*   *   *

F RANK learned that 421 Squadron had returned to Kenley only two weeks earlier, having spent all of August, all of September and half of October in the Kent countryside. They had lived under canvas — first near a small town called Lashendon in Kent, and then at another small town called Headcorn. All activities were accommodated in tents or in modified Bedford trucks. Squadron commander offices, for instance, were housed in the canvas-covered back of a Bedford truck. Intelligence/operations consisted of two Bedford trucks backed up close to each other with canvas coverings strung up between. Everything else, from the sick bay to the officer's mess, was housed in a tent. The pilots slept on camp cots in an assortment of two-man or four-man tents. The runways were grass fields overlain by a steel mesh called Somerfeldt tracking. The wing moved twice and the second time was much better than the first. They improved the time it took to complete the move and the smoothness of the operation. With the onset of winter, the wing happily moved one more time, but this time into the warmth and comfort of barracks buildings at RAF Station Kenley. Because of the motivation of warm 'digs', this move was better again by far. They came in from the cold 14 October.

Frank reported to the squadron along with another pilot F/O 'Scotty' McRoberts. The following is the entry in the squadron Operations Record Book (ORB) for 29 October 1943, the date when the postings were conveyed to the squadron:

> "Weather again foggy, and not a single sortie was flown during the day. Two pilots, F/L F J Clark and F/O R C McRoberts have been posted to this squadron for flying duties effective today. Fifty dozen Christmas cards have been ordered to meet the requirements of the personnel of 421 Squadron. There was a cinema show 'San Francisco' in the Officer's Mess in the evening."

His new squadron was a source of great delight for Frank — it was all he could have wanted. Kenley was one of the major aerodromes in the ring that surrounded London and from the first moments of the war, was a busy place — full of action either launching fighter aircraft to the attack or being attacked by the enemy. Kenley was bombed numerous times by German aircraft that crossed the south coast near Brighton, picked up the railroad line and followed it north until they were at Whyteleafe Railroad Station. There, on a highland above the station was RAF Station Kenley. One of these raids, in August 1940, was a massive attack by hundreds of German aircraft in several waves that resulted in widespread damage, the loss of more than a dozen aircraft, the lives of 10 personnel and three times that number injured.

Frank arrived feeling considerable humility because he had heard of the great 'Red Indian' Squadron — one of the top fighter squadrons in the European theatre. He met the squadron commander, S/L Chuck Magwood, who greeted him, gave him some background about the squadron and introduced him to his new boss, F/L 'Web' Harten, commander of 'A' Flight. Harten introduced him to the other members of 'A' Flight. It was then that he learned that F/O Andy MacKenzie — who was Bev Baily's cousin — was in 'B' Flight along with F/L Wally Quint, a fellow who had been part of the instruction staff at Aylmer while Frank was there. Among the ground crew were two ex-West Hillians, John Sancton who was an engineering officer with the wing headquarters staff and Monty Berger who was the Chief Intelligence Officer. Frank immediately started questioning whoever would give him time, trying to learn all the details of this famous squadron's history and the names of all the present and past heroes who had brought it to its present status. His enthusiasm shows through in the letter he wrote to Bev Baily:

"X Unit

RAF Station Kenley
Surrey
2 November 1943
Dear old Joe,

Just a few lines to keep you posted as to my whereabouts. Incidentally, thanks muchly for your last letter of 7 October which up to now I have not received. Might as well tell you the big news first — I'm happy at last! I finally got my posting last Thursday and am now the second junior member of 421 Squadron — you've probably heard or read of it as the 'Red Indian' Squadron. It is cracked up to be a pretty bloody good squadron and is in a wing which right now stands highest in

Fighter Command. So am feeling very honoured and bloody thrilled to have the opportunity of being part of it. Incidentally, your cousin Andy MacKenzie is in the squadron too. He's been with it for about three months now and already has one to his credit — as you can see they don't waste any time in 421. There are an awful lot of chaps here that I have known at various times in my young life, including a couple of chaps who used to instruct with me at Aylmer and John Sancton (editor of Annual 1937) and Monty Berger both ex-West Hillians. So I feel pretty much at home.

We're flying the same type of kite I flew at my OTU but a much more modern version — even much more modern than the ones Tommy is flying. So in all respects I'm very happy about the whole deal. Will most likely have done some trips before I see you next, so will have much to talk over.

By the way, when the hell am I going to see you again? If I was correct in following the moves you expected to make in your last letter, I imagine you should be ending up somewhere around where I am, shortly. You should be able to pin-point me from my address. I think you mentioned in your letter that you wouldn't be free until about the middle of this month. I might be able to wangle a couple of days by then. But really I don't want to ask for much leave from here for a while yet as I am a junior in the squadron and all that and besides I don't want to miss any trips if I can help it. Want to get as much experience and gen on Jerry as I can before next spring.

My time at Bournemouth was very enjoyable and I had a bloody good time despite the fact that I got awfully brassed at times. It cost me a fortune there though. I joined three private drinking clubs where I had all my good times but they were a bit expensive. I actually left Bournemouth last Thursday — posted to another refresher course (to keep my hand in while waiting) at Tommy's old OTU (remember when you and I went to visit him?) I just got up there when I was notified of my posting to 421 so back down I came again the next day. Opened my bottle of rye on the train coming down to celebrate the happy occasion — but there is still half of it left. If it's not too long before I see you again, you may still be able to have a snort. We had a wild bloody trip up to Grangemouth — Brownie and Mac (you met him at Daniel O'Connor School) and I went up there together. We got completely corned before we left Bournemouth. And had a two-hour stop in London where we sopped up more like three sponges at the

Brevet Club. As a result I left my laundry in Bournemouth and lost my respirator and a haversack somewhere along the route. Brownie was posted down here with me, so I did have some company when I cracked the rye. The one night I had at Grangemouth was another glorious piss-up — on rum too. So my posting was certainly well celebrated.

Have you got that razor from Gerry yet? I can appreciate your former difficulties now, as I lost mine in the haversack. However, figure I should grow a beard anyway with winter creeping on apace.

Well let's hear from you when you get a chance and let's start making plans for Xmas now, besides trying to get together sooner. Cheers

Frankie"

The Commanding Officer of 421 Squadron, S/L C M 'Chuck' Magwood, led the squadron for a mere two months. During this time the squadron had been very active indeed — October was the best month in the squadron's history. In five engagements, 3 October, 18 October, 22 October, 24 October and 25 October, they claimed the destruction of eight enemy fighter aircraft and the damaging of six others for the loss of only two of their own 421 pilots. One of the two pilots — F/O W F Bill 'Cookie' Cook — parachuted into northern France, evaded capture from the enemy, contacted the French Underground, and returned via one of the secret exit routes through Spain to Gibraltar and thence to England. Cookie returned and visited the squadron just before Christmas on his way to a welcome return to Canada for a leave. The other pilot who was lost — F/S Ian Forster — was not so fortunate, he was shot down and killed in the last engagement of the month.

The active October was a continuation of a very busy summer for 421 Squadron. The squadron was formed in April 1942, but nearly a year was spent in training and quasi-operational activities such as coastal convoy patrols. By January 1943 the squadron was considered ready for operations and they moved to Kenley exchanging their Mark V Spitfires for the Mark IX Spitfires of 416 Squadron. But it was June 1943, when S/L Buck McNair took over as commanding officer, things started to happen. McNair had proven to be an excellent fighter pilot in Malta where he flew with such pilots as Buzz Beurling, Wally

McLeod, Johnny Sherlock, Johnny McElroy and Claud Weaver. McNair had eight victories, five probable victories and ten enemy aircraft damaged to his credit when he arrived back in the UK from Malta. He was soon made commander of 416 Squadron and then hurriedly transferred to command 421 upon the tragic loss of Phil Archer. Archer was a West Indian, greatly respected by all and the squadron looked forward to his coming to lead them. Unfortunately he was killed in a dogfight shortly after taking command. McNair, rushed in to fill the vacancy, not only replaced Archer but ignited the neophyte and barely experienced 421 Squadron with daring strikes that inspired everyone. In the course of this exciting time he personally destroyed another eight enemy aircraft while his eager pilots accounted for 11 others. McNair became the highest-scoring pilot in 421 Squadron history. The squadron history states:

> "On the eleventh of October S/L McNair was awarded a second bar to his DFC and was promoted out of the squadron to the W/C's job five days later. S/L Charles Magwood, DFC, with a record of four-and-one-tenth enemy aircraft destroyed, and two-and-one-half damaged, assumed command. His tenure was short, with not much activity after October, and he was posted out on the thirteenth of December."

Within four days of Frank's arrival there was another dogfight. With 30 pilots and only 18 aircraft on the roster in 421 Squadron, it took a while for a new arrival to be slotted into the rotation. Frank was still flying training sessions, learning the details of squadron battle tactics and hence was not assigned to fly that day. His first turn would come three weeks later. But witnessing the exuberance of the successful pilots that night in the Officer's Mess undoubtedly made him feel envious and proud of his unit. The squadron made the following report entered into the ORB for 3 November 1943:

> "Weather good, and the squadron took part in Ramrod 289 — up 1003 hours, down 1200 hours. The squadron encountered considerable action with enemy casualties as follows — lone FW 190 destroyed by S/L C M Magwood DFC — one FW 190 destroyed and one Me 109 damaged by F/L F J Sherlock and one Me 109 probably destroyed by F/L A E Fleming. Several of our aircraft landed at advanced bases."

Frank was so interested in what the participants had to say at the bar that he chased down Monty Berger and asked to read the Combat Report that was submitted to Fighter Command Headquarters describing the aerial battle. These Top Secret documents were not normally handed about, but Monty agreed to let Frank read this one. Here is what he read†:

"GENERAL REPORT: 24 Spitfires IX of 127 (Fighter) Wing led by S/L C M Magwood, DFC, flying with 421 Squadron acted as top cover to 72 Marauders bombing St André de L'Eure aerodrome. The wing was airborne at 1003 hours, made rendezvous with the bombers, who were late and off-course in mid-channel and proceeded to the target which was accurately bombed. Sticks of bombs were seen on the north and south dispersal buildings and two large fires broke out in the northern corner of the field. The majority of the wing had landed safely at base by 1200 hours, but six aircraft put down at various forward aerodromes due to shortage of petrol.

Shortly after crossing the Seine, just north of Evreux, smoke trails were sighted to the south flying westward at about 26,000 feet a little above 403, the top squadron. The wing climbed to 30,000 feet and gave chase but the enemy aircraft, about 12 to 15 unidentified, reached 32,000 feet while flying southward and about the target area turned inland and disappeared. The wing then lost height turning to port and saw the bombers immediately below on their bombing run, seeing many good bursts a few seconds later. As the bombers were turning port and heading out, a large gaggle of Me 109s approached from the east. At the same time, 403 Squadron sighted a gaggle of FW 190s at 9 o'clock above them.

Black and Green Sections of 421 Squadron went down on the rear of the gaggle of about 15 Me 109s and White Section broke into some 10 FW 190s. The general melée then began with 403 Squadron maintaining top cover for 421."

"F/L FLEMING: I was flying Green 1 and attacked the last of 15 enemy aircraft that passed. They came down from smoke-trail height (26,000 feet) across our front and turned starboard diving slightly. I turned sharply starboard and followed the last aircraft, an Me 109G.

---

† Intelligence Form "F" Report dated 3 November 1943 and appended to 421 Squadron ORB reel C-12295, National Archives and Library of Canada.

I fired two short intervals from approximately 400 yards with no result. About 2 minutes later, having lost his speed of initial dive, I closed and fired several bursts from 250 to 70 yards, almost dead astern. His evasive action was slight. I observed strikes on fuselage and right wing root; pieces of enemy aircraft flew off and one hit my aircraft knocking the cowling off my starboard cannon. I broke off and orbitted twice at 8,000 feet observing enemy aircraft diving steeply towards the ground. He entered cloud at approximately 2,000 feet still diving. No smoke or fire was seen. I claim one Me 109G probably destroyed."

"F/L SHERLOCK (White 2): The wing leader (Black 1) dived to attack one formation and White Section climbed to attack the other Jerry formation. As I was overtaking the formation, a Me 109 pulled out of the gaggle and climbed steeply into the sun. As he was trying to get behind us I broke away from White 1 and attacked him firing a 2-to-3-second burst from about 500 yards. I hit him with my first shots and due to my speed falling off, I could not hold him in my sights and finally spun off the attack. I claim this Me 109 damaged. ... I again climbed up into the sun and saw several 190s below. All but one half-rolled, so I turned on him. He broke into me head-on but after a steep climbing turn I again attacked him firing a long burst. He half-rolled, did a couple of flick rolls and then aileron-dived down. I again fired a long burst at him, several pieces of his aircraft coming off. At about 15,000 feet he emitted a lot of black smoke and I broke off the attack. At 10,000 feet he

Figure 11 — Frank standing with Mae West on at the door to the 421 Squadron dispersal hut at Kenley.

(Baily collection)

was still spinning down and as there were still a lot of 190s above, I again climbed up and did not see if he crashed."

P/O DeCourcy of 421, submitted a report confirming that he saw Sherlock's victim crash. F/O Findley and F/O Middlemiss of 403 Squadron reported that they saw two white parachutes far below them north-west of the target. After the battle, while the scattered Spitfires were assembling near the coast trying to recover their protective escort for the bombers, S/L Magwood saw a single 190 try to attack the bombers well below. He dove, gathered considerable speed and rapidly overtook the attacker and with a 3-second burst from 300 to 175 yards saw him burst into smoke and crash in a field. The pilot did not bale out. F/L Monty Berger summarized the total engagement as follows:

"OUR CASUALTIES: nil

ENEMY CASUALTIES:

1 FW 190 destroyed by S/L Magwood — 80 cannon, 332 MG rounds, cine camera used

1 FW 190 destroyed by F/L Sherlock

1 Me 109 damaged by F/L Sherlock — 225 cannon, 1000 MG rounds, cine camera used

1 Me 109 probably destroyed by F/L Fleming
cine camera used — 195 cannon, 1240 MG rounds."

This was the stuff of being a fighter pilot. Frank could see the whole battle in his mind's eye. How he wished he could sit down and write an exact account of the aerial battle in a letter to Joe Baily, but for security reasons he could not. What he dreamed was that the next one would see him as a participant.

Each front-line squadron commander knew the essential need to establish a fighting style and a discipline to every tactic from responding to a 'bounce' that could come from any quarter to the many variations of wheeling, climbing or diving to implement an attack. This took a lot of practise and a good squadron commander had to continuously lead his men into training sessions, drilling the routines — much like football plays — until each pilot could anticipate what the leader was going to do before he did it. Frank lined up as much flying time as he could and threw himself into learning the fighting style and discipline of his newly adopted squadron. And when he wasn't flying practise flights with one or two other pilots he was keenly following as S/L Magwood led the whole squadron in the training flights — turns, banks and attacks. Frank was determined to become totally proficient in all these tactics.

At last his moment came. Nearly three weeks after the aerial battle described, his name was posted on the list of pilots who would fly on a mission the following day. That night Frank hardly slept. Tossing and turning he was excited and thrilled at the prospect of aerial combat, but the nagging doubt of his ability to handle the fear turned his stomach, gave him a headache and caused disruption in his bowels. If this is what he was now, how could he handle the hour before take-off? Let alone an actual combat?

The morning of 23 November came and curiously, the early hours before dawn had been much worse than dawn itself. His stomach and innards had settled sufficiently for breakfast and even though he was not going to take off until two in the afternoon, he cruised through the morning and noon in relative calm concentrating on the fact that this is what he had trained for, longed for and now would taste.

The mission was called 'Ramrod 325', and Frank flew Red 2 — wing man to his flight leader, F/L Web Harten. F/L Johnny Sherlock flew Red 3 with P/O Bill Barnett his wingman. This was to be a fighter escort of Boston and Mitchell medium bombers that were to bomb a pilotless bomb site in a Belgian woods near the coast, while the fighters would escort them and hope to flush out a few enemy fighters. As the truck took the pilots out to the dispersal hut, Frank was as excited as a small boy at a picnic. He could see the mission turning into one like the combat report he had read. Although there were butterflies, he calmed himself down, did his pre-flight check, urinated at the back of the aircraft and hopped in as he had so many times before.

Frank concentrated on making a perfect take-off and staying at the exact spot off Web Harten's wing where he should be. He flew with the wing south-east from Kenley, where they rendezvoused with the medium bombers of No. 2 Group out in the Channel. Then the whole entourage dropped down to wave-top level below German radar and headed for the French coast. The 24 Spitfires of 127 Wing crossed the coast at Hardelot (ten miles south of Boulogne), climbed to 15,000 feet, turned due east and flew protective cover over the pilotless bomb site. The bombers hammered the target, and when they headed back to the coast, the fighters swept the area from St. Omer south-east 20 miles (32 kilometres) to Bethune (near Dunkirk). They flew over the airfield, turned south-west 40 miles (64 kilometres) to sweep Abbeville, and finally flew due north to Le Touquet. It was on this return flight that they encountered some light flak when crossing the coast at Le Touquet, but it was about a half-mile away and was more like distant fireworks. Frank watched for it to come closer for he knew they were really firing at him! Soon he had passed out of range of the flak centre. He saw it, recognized the moment as the great test that experienced pilots described and broke out into a broad smile. It had been a very light exposure because the flak was far away, but he had felt the rush of panic and immediately damped it down. He knew he had yet to encounter the real thing — close at hand — but he also knew he could handle it.

The two squadrons encountered no other opposition on the whole 350 mile route and they landed at Kenley one-hour-and-thirty-five-minutes after take-off. What a disappointment! The ORB reported:

> "The weather finally cleared up this morning and after six days inactivity the squadron took off at 1440 hours on Ramrod 325. The trip was uneventful and our aircraft returned at 1615 hours."

It may have seemed uneventful to the Intelligence Officer who submitted the official trip report and the Adjutant who inscribed it in the squadron diary, but to Frank it was a dream come true. Firstly, because of the sheer panic when the first flak started exploding — even if it was a half-mile away — and the butterflies in his stomach when they began the flight didn't really go away until they were letting down at home base. His mind was in a whirl from take-off to landing, caught up in the pure delight of doing the real thing — a combat operation that he had been training for and dreaming about for over three years. But at the same time he recognized how terrifying it had been.

Abbeville and the immediate surrounds had long been the home base of JG 26[†] — the famous yellow-nosed German fighter squadrons that were extremely experienced and devastating in combat. They were, after all, the home group of Alfred Galland — perhaps the best known German fighter ace. It came as a great surprise to Frank that there was no opposition over the home bases of this famous group of wings. What the Germans knew and the Allies didn't was that the build-up of Allied forces attacking Europe daily was so great that the Luftwaffe would only commit aircraft in battle when it knew it had a clear numerical advantage.

Frank flew again on the 25 November on Ramrod 333 when they took off in early afternoon with 403 and 421 Squadrons escorting Mitchells and Mosquitos bombing another pilotless bomb site at Audinghem and then sweeping the Cambrai, Amiens and Abbeville area. The area was thick with bases for such Luftwaffe fighter units as JG 1, JG 5, JG 11, JG 26 and JG 53. The official intelligence account says the Ramrod was uneventful, but there must have been at least one long-distance exchange of fire with an enemy aircraft, for in a letter written 22 December, Frank says, "... had one abortive attempt but doubt very much if I even scared him let alone hit him." This occurred just before he got sick.

That afternoon, "a captured FW 190 accompanied by two Spitfires from the field, took part in a shootout over the airfield witnessed by a large number of interested spectators."[‡]

What a display! Frank's blood bubbled watching the simulated dogfight as it swirled up high, ebbed and then came closer in ever-decreasing turns until it blasted across the airfield. This was the best possible sample of what was about to become his career.

---

† JG stood for Jagdgeschader 'hunter' group. It consisted of several wings (in the RAF scheme of things). I./JG 26 flying FW 190s was the equivalent of an RAF wing, but there was also II./JG 26 flying Me 109s and III./JG 26 flying FW 190s — all part of the same aeronautical assemblage.

‡ 421 Squadron ORB — 25 November.

Figure 12 — Frank (second from left in the back row) and F/L Bob Middlemiss of 403 Squadron (far right in the back row) accompanied by six members of the ground crew scouted for turkeys for Christmas dinner. The Warrant Officer at lower right is warning the turkey of what is in store for it.

(CF Photo PL26275)

But just as he thought his fighting career was about to begin, disappointment struck. Three days after his second operational mission, he was admitted to hospital suffering a severe bout of the flu. Frank was discharged from hospital days later, but was advised to lay low for a few days. The foul weather caused half the pilots in the squadron to come down sick. More bad weather set in shutting down all flying and before better weather returned, Frank had a recurrence of the flu that grounded him until the end of December. The squadron ORB entry for 12 December states:

> "Weather still very dull with poor visibility. Squadron still at Bradwell Bay. F/L F J Clark has been ordered away on 14 days sick leave by the Squadron Medical Officer".

From mid-December through the early part of January the squadron was plagued with illness — most often flu. But it was plagued by a management problem as well. The three top officers in the squadron were all approaching 'End of Tour' (EOT) at the same time. Chuck Magwood, the squadron commander, was slated to be put behind a desk 13 December, while his two lieutenants Web Harten and Al Fleming, commanders of 'A' and 'B' Flights, were to be relieved the following day. Luckily, there was an internal candidate in Karl Linton who could take over 'A' Flight. The solution was to find replacements from 403 Squadron — Magwood to be replaced by Jimmy Lambert and Ed Gimbel to replace Fleming. 403 Squadron had such depth that it could provide these two fine airmen to 421.

While Frank was away in the hospital, the squadron experienced a severe jolt. On 20 December, on Ramrod 375 that was supposed to be a sweep of the area between Douai and Lille, 421 Squadron was flying about 12,000 feet whilst 403 Squadron was flying high cover at 20,000 feet when they encountered 18 Me 109s of I./JG 3 over Merville, five miles (8 kilometres) west of Lille. S/L Jimmy Lambert, F/L Karl Linton and F/L Andy MacKenzie each claimed a Me 109 destroyed (although subsequently, MacKenzie's claim was reduced to a 'probably destroyed') and Linton claimed two others damaged. But before 403 could join in, 421 Squadron was bounced by 20 FW 190s of I./JG 26. Lambert was shot down and killed in the bounce, but the squadron recovered in a fury and MacKenzie claimed two, F/L Ed Gimbel claimed one, F/O Tommy DeCourcy claimed one and as the battle came to a close, F/O Bob Pentland of 403 Squadron claimed one damaged FW 190. The victory by 421 Squadron of seven destroyed and two damaged came at the expense of their new commander — Lambert was shot down and killed. He was a highly regarded flight commander in 403 Squadron who took leave to get married on the third of December. So popular was he that pilots from 403, 421 and several other RCAF squadrons attended the wedding in Scotland. It was while on his honeymoon, that Lambert learned he was being transferred from 403 Squadron and promoted to the rank of S/L to succeed S/L Chuck Magwood. Lambert returned on the thirteenth of December but the weather was bad enough to prohibit any operations for a week. On the first occasion when Lambert could lead an operational mission under his new command, he was killed. It was a horrible shock. Squadron records, trying to play down the tragedy to keep morale high, summarized the encounter as follows:

"The weather has finally cleared, and everyone agrees it is very nice to see blue sky again. At 2015 hours the Squadron took off on Ramrod 375. Approximately 38 enemy aircraft were encountered and 421 Squadron chalked up a remarkable score of seven destroyed and two damaged for the loss of one, S/L J F Lambert. F/O A R MacKenzie destroyed two FW 190s and one Me 109, F/L E L Gimbel DFC destroyed one FW 190, and F/L K R Linton destroyed one Me 109 and damaged two, P/O T J DeCourcy destroyed one FW 190 and S/L J F Lambert destroyed one Me 109. This was the first operation that S/L J F Lambert had led 421 Squadron. He was a very popular Commanding Officer and will be greatly missed."

After a few days, the squadron learned that Jimmy Lambert's replacement to lead the squadron was to be S/L W A G 'Wally' Conrad who was on leave in Canada. Conrad was well known to the pilots because he had briefly been the commander of 403 Squadron in August 1943 when the two squadrons operated from

Figure 13 — F/O Andy MacKenzie sporting the newly-earned DFC he was awarded for three victories claimed 20 December 1943.

(McElroy collection)

grass fields. Conrad first flew with an RAF squadron in North Africa and returned to the UK in May 1943 to fly with 403 Squadron. He rose to command 403 Squadron, but five days after taking over, Conrad was on a mission engaged in a close battle with a FW 190 over France when he and his wingman collided. His aircraft broke into pieces and he managed to get out of the cockpit section at very low altitude. His parachute streamed when he baled out, but he was saved by landing in a huge haystack although he lost a shoe in the process. Conrad evaded capture and with the help of the French Underground returned to England via Spain. In December he had a much-deserved leave in Canada and reported to 421 Squadron in early January. In the meantime, F/L E L 'Ed' Gimbel, an American from Chicago who crossed the border into Canada, trained in the BCATP and served with 401 Squadron in 1942, became acting squadron commander. Ed Gimbel will come into our narrative again a few months later on — in a most bazaar way.

Frank's letter to Bev says little about these events because the censors were pretty tough on that sort of thing:

"421 Squadron
RCAF England
Wed 22 Dec 1943

Dear old Joe

Fine thing! — sneaking off on the hush, without so much as a farewell binge, to the ho-ho-lands — or are you sloshing around in the muddy beauty of Italy? I really don't expect an answer to that as I know you probably can't say for security reasons. Well it looks like we both finally got what we've wanted for so long, Joe, a chance for some action — one big push. Received your very thoughtful Xmas Airgraph this morning. Thanks awfully, Joe. I'm afraid my Xmas greetings won't catch up with you till next Xmas as I didn't know for sure where you were till I got your Airgraph this morning. Anyway, late as it may be — I hope you had a very good Xmas, Joe, and all my best wishes go to you for the New Year — lots of luck too, boy.

I got my posting to 421 Squadron about the end of October and shortly after began to hear rumours from Tommy and Ken and from home that you had left England so haven't written (except for a Xmas card) since then 'til I could get hold of your address. I've been on some 'shows' but haven't had a decent crack at a 'Jerry' yet — had one abortive attempt but doubt very much if I even scared him let alone hit him. Then I caught the flu and have been grounded for the last month. Just finished a final week of sick leave at Chester and hope to be serviceable for flying again after my medical board tomorrow. There are a damn keen bunch of fellows here as it is an all-Canadian wing — including your cousin Andy MacKenzie, who by the way has four destroyed to his credit. He's doing damn fine and shouldn't be surprised to see him 'gonged' shortly — great tribe these Bailys!

Tommy has been taken off ops and has been given a job as an instructor, which has really infuriated him. Ken is on a ship now — HMS Indefatiguable (add c/o GRO London and that's his address). Tommy's address is No. 2 FIS Montrose, Scotland, till about January — but I guess straight 'RCAF, England' would be safest. None of us are going to be able to get together for Xmas so you're not going to be missing a 'Joe Session'. Reports from home are very encouraging and I hear from the wife that Mary still loves you (silly girl), incidentally the wife still seems to love me (silly girl). The young son is progressing favourably; showing radicalist tendencies, disinclination to walk altho he's quite a going concern on 'all fours'; and attributes his success to his enlightened and in all respects brilliant father.

Am planning on a very boozy Xmas binge, followed by an even boozier New Years binge and my greatest regret is that you won't be here to binge with. However on the stroke of the last midnight of 1943 there will be at least one brimming glass of spirits drunk, with a feeling of friendship and respect, to the toast 'Success to Temperance'. Cheers.

Frankie"

On Christmas day, the officers threw a great big party for the children from the neighbouring village in the Officer's Mess — serving them turkeys Frank and the others had acquired. To the merriment of the children and all the airmen at Kenley, Santa Claus came flying into the airfield in a Tiger Moth, which was painted white and marked 'North Pole Express'. Frank was back in good health by Christmas day. The spirits of all at Kenley were high as every effort was made to make Christmas dinner special in spite of the shortage of almost every kind of foodstuffs in the UK in 1943.

Frank and two other pilots were on ten-minute readiness five days later when, at 1110 hours, the urgent command 'Scramble!' blasted out of the Tannoy loudspeakers. Frank, Karl Linton and Scotty McRoberts took off immediately into a clear but very cold, blue sky. They climbed at full power anxiously expecting some action, roamed over the area vectored by ground control but found nothing. It was a false alarm. That was disappointing, but it was made even more so when there was a great deal of celebration and excitement in the Officer's Mess that night when it was learned that two 403 Squadron pilots each claimed shooting down a Me 109.

That night he wrote two long letters to Bev:

"421 squadron
RCAF England
30 December 1943 number 1

Dear old Joe,

After about a month of sporadic and disappointing mail reception I got a bloody wonderful surprise this morning in the form of two

letters from you — an Airgraph dated 8 December and short note
with a photo of you enclosed dated 12 December. Thanks awfully
for taking time to write, Joe, and especially for the photo — pretty
bloody glamourous and yet it still looks like you. Just back from a
'Scramble' on which we saw SFA except a few pretty little cloudlettes
which were far from hostile — so your letters lifted me right back up
into the blue after the anti-climax of such a show. Have just finished
lunch and may have to beat my ass back down to dispersal before
I finish this — but will take it with me and finish it down there if
necessary. First of all, Joe, let me repeat how bloody wonderful it is
to hear from you. Without getting too involved I can simply say I've
missed seeing you and being able to contact you like bloody hell. It
was a hell of a goddam shock when I got a letter from Kenny saying
he thought you had gone out East — there were so many future leaves
I had sort of dimly planned for our mutual fun and games, but 'the
best laid plans of mice and men oft gang astray' — which sounds
awfully philosophical and all that rot but still doesn't remedy things
much. It sure was a disappointment to me although I imagine you
must be bloody happy about your move, but thank God we're young,
Joe, and have lots of years ahead of us after the war to look forward to.
What a pack of yarns we're going to have to exchange at that Victory
Binge at the Normandie Roof. Hope you're as fit as you look in the
picture, as good health is a hell of a good thing to have (and be able to
maintain) when you're facing old Jerry — especially the boys you're
going to run up against. Have been following the Italian Campaign a
hell of a lot closer since I found out you're down in that area. There's
not much of a chance of our heading down that way — our move, if it
ever comes, will be due east. Since the Teheran Conference, England
has been simply buzzing with invasion talk — the papers say the
Yanks are now involved in the greatest manoeuvres ever staged in
England as they will form about 73% of the invasion forces. We have
been a mobile airfield for quite some time now and could push off
any time anywhere. And as the talk goes, something is going to come
of it and public opinion says March — which of course is neither here
nor there really, but it all goes to make life a bit more exciting and
ennervating as expectation always does.

You asked for news from Canada which I won't have room to include
in this but which I'll devote another form to as soon as I finish this.
Now that I know the mail set-up with you and that my letters reach
you much quicker than Canadian mail, I'll keep a letter or two on

the way all the time with bits of gen I pick up from Junie's letters. Conditions down there from your letters sound pretty wonderful — oranges, Canadian beer, Dewar's scotch, champagne, wine, nuts, etc. but then that's only the bright side of it all I imagine. Still I envy you like hell as it must be a wonderful experience even seeing the Med and Sicily and all the other countries you have or will see under war conditions. And besides all that, the action you've wanted for so damn long is now just around the corner. Yes, I can imagine how much you must have enjoyed your trip down and how you are and will be enjoying your changed routine of life down there, even in spite of the many little inconveniences like slow mail service, that try like hell to pull a fellow down into gloom from the normal exuberance that such wonderful experiences make for you. Yes sir, Joe if you're not (which I doubt) you should be having yourself one hell of time. The old hackneyed phrase 'wish I were with you' is certainly in order right now. Was sorry as hell we couldn't get together for Xmas, Joe, spent mine in a drunken sort of bliss, right on the station. Could have had leave, but Sicily is one hell of a long way away. Incidentally I'm all over the flu and back on ops again. Andy MacKenzie, who is also in 421 Squadron has four German aircraft to his credit. He's quite a hero — more about him in the next letter. Hope you get them both together. Cheers! and lots of luck — Frankie."

"30 Dec 1943 number 2

Dear old Joe,

Have just finished one of those forms to you but found there wasn't quite enough room to accommodate what I wanted to say, so am continuing on this. Hope the two reach you together. I finished the other talking of Andy MacKenzie. Well he's been with 421 Squadron since last July and got his first Hun in October some time. He was the first person I saw when I walked into the Mess here just after arriving. Just a short while ago the wing was out on a do and ran into a mess of Fock Wolfe 190s. Old Andy barged right into them and shot down three which is almost a bloody record for single-engined aircraft — at one time I mean. It was a damn fine show and we're all expecting him to get the DFC out of it. Can't tell you much about the station I'm on, Joe, except that it is comfortable and has a bloody fine Mess with a whole big room made into a bar, other gen about our work, aircraft, set-up, etc. as you know is highly secret — to everybody but the old

Jerries I sometimes think. We're handy to London and life goes on at a really fast and furious pace around here. You always find that on an operational station, and even more so on fighter stations for some reason or other. Anyway, it's a hell of a nice way to live when you're away from home and your friends — you're too absorbed with the present to let your mind linger too much on the past or the future.

Speaking of home — things seem to be going on in the usual way from what I gather from Junie's letters in any case. June Healy was married a couple of weeks ago to a very nice young chap from all reports. Ernie and Jean, as you probably know by now, are getting married next June. They already have an apartment picked out which will be theirs in May, giving them a month to fix it up before moving in. Looks like you're next after them, Joe. Yours should be a bang-up affair as all the Joes should be home by then to help you say I do. You won't lack for advice anyway, Joe, with Ernie and I behind you busting with the pride of our married status. Mary was up to visit your Mom and Dad recently and Junie saw her again. The opinions of all the folks back home are still and promise to be always, 100% 'pro-Mary'. Your Mom and Dad very kindly remembered me at Xmas with some bloody wonderful candy which was really thoughtful of them. I sent home the pictures that Kenny and I took while on our 'big four' leave and Junie always takes whatever pictures she gets from me up to your mother. From there they usually go the rounds. The winter seems to be a typical one back in Montreal — snow and lots of sub-zero weather — makes me pine for the old skiing days. We're going to have lots of fun skiing after the war Joe, with our crutches and peg-legs and stumpy arms. The mothers and girls get together every once in a while at tea-parties etc, and talk of their wonderful sons, husbands or sweeties. The last one was at Mrs Smith's. Had a letter from old Joe Mills recently and he was full of the impending hitching-party for he and Jeanie. By golly they deserve all the happiness in the world. Ernie's been damned swell to Junie and I by taking pictures of Barry every so often for Junie to send over to me. The Palins have had another short note from Kerle. It arrived just before Xmas and must have made their Xmas an awful lot brighter. Haven't heard much about Bill since he left to join the navy. The Navy Show, that he's in, has been a thumping success right across Canada.

Got most of my Xmas parcels yesterday (imagine you haven't had yours even by the time you receive this) and they included a parcel from good old Brampton which had a bottle of Seagram's 83 tucked inside. By golly, I wish you were here to help me kill this one — but don't feel too bad about drinking it myself seeing as how you're getting Canadian beer and scotch. Still it's not drinking the stuff that counts, it's who you drink it with. By the by, there must be a few things that you'll be needing that you can't get in Sicily — please let me know what they are, Joe, and I'll send them on to you at once if I can get them in this country. Soap or cigarettes I could send immediately if you need them as I have a large supply on hand — much more than I need.

Haven't heard from Tom or Ken since I wrote you last the twenty-second. Interested to hear that you saw Harry Harrison's young brother — I saw Harry Harrison about a month ago at Bournemouth where I went for a 48. I took him and a couple of his friends up to a club I belonged to there and did a bit of drinking. So Norm Taylor's down there too, eh? I hear Hal Carstairs is too. Would be interesting if you could contact. He may not be in Sicily though. Haven't had any real recent news from home for quite a while as the mail over here has been held up due to Xmas rush. Will keep you posted as often as I can though when the mail gets a bit more regular. Well, Joe, look after yourself and don't take too many chances — remember 'discretion is the better part of valour'. Write when you can as I really enjoy hearing from you. All the best.

Frankie"

The next day, ushering out the old year 1943, Frank flew on Ramrod 403 — another wing-strength sweep of the Cambrai area while escorting medium bombers directed against pilotless bomb sites. All-in-all there were five Ramrods flown by the 2ndTAF against such sites that day — each one a wing-strength fighter support to Mitchells or Marauders. Then in the afternoon there were eight more sweeps by various RAF squadrons. The Allies were stepping up activities.

Frank spotted only one enemy aircraft on the Ramrod, but it was too far away to intercept, so the squadron flew on, performed their sweep and on the way home observed a new pilotless bomb site not previously reported but already heavily scarred with bomb craters. They returned to Kenley at 1450 hours and at the de-briefing received some information from 2ndTAF headquarters at Uxbridge that in all the operations to mid-day there had been no Luftwaffe opposition but that two Typhoons were lost due to mid-air collision in the middle of the Channel.

Chapter Five

BEFORE the year ended, Frank received word that he had qualified by two months for a Ribbon and Star awarded to all military personnel who served operationally in the 1939 to 1943 period of conflict. He received his Star the first of January 1944. The intention was to issue a further award for those engaging in the new — and hopefully final — phase of the war that would include the build-up, the actual invasion of the continent and the march into Germany to bring about the final destruction of the Nazis.

Figure 14 — S/L Wally Conrad, DFC, served a complete tour in North Africa and was starting another when, in mid-August 1943, he and his wing man collided over Europe. Conrad parachuted, evaded and was smuggled through France and Spain to Gibraltar. After a good rest in Canada, he took over command of 421 Squadron in January 1944. Conrad was credited with five enemy aircraft destroyed and three shared.

(CF Photo PL26562)

In addition to the award, New Years Day saw the arrival of the new commander, S/L W A G 'Wally' Conrad. Many pilots knew Wally for he had flown with, and eventually commanded the sister-squadron 403 the previous summer.

Frank was healthy again and eager to fly, but he had only flown four missions — two at the end of November and two on the last two days of December. He was due for his first pilot evaluation review, but first he had a mission to fly. A total of eight Ramrods were planned by 2ndTAF for 4 January 1944; 127 Wing was to fly two of them — one to Boulogne in the morning and the other to Dieppe in early afternoon. Frank flew White 2, wing man to Karl Linton on Ramrod 416 led by Ed Gimbel. On the way to the site there was intense heavy flak over Boulogne, but Frank handled it well, barely flinching as the black puffs of smoke and blinding flashes approached their section but veered off and were soon past. Minutes later they were over the pilotless bomb site where the bombers they were escorting, unloaded. At the completion of the bomb run, 403 Squadron strafed the site setting several nisson huts ablaze while 421 provided high cover.

It was with considerable trepidation that Frank waited for Wally Conrad to come back from the second Ramrod to sit down to complete his performance evaluation. Conrad didn't know Frank very well and had conferred with Ed Gimbel and Web Harten to give him some insight. Wally gave Frank very good ratings for the part of the review that dealt with personal characteristics — appearance, creativity, diligence, sociability, etc., but Wally had to defer judgement in that far more critical part of the evaluation, how a pilot performed in action. There had not been enough operational flying to properly assess such categories as leadership, readiness to engage in battle, performance under combat stress and discipline under fire. This latter part of the review accounted for 60% of the total rating and so Frank was disappointed with a score of only 44, but he recognized it to be fair. His consolation was that when he expressed his disappointment to Wally, that old veteran — fully one year older than Frank — said to him, "Frank, the toughest part of becoming a good fighter pilot is to master the instincts of knowing when to slip, when to bunt and to know the exact moment to pull off a split-S. But even more important, one has to learn to read the big picture — what the brass has in mind, how they try to deploy our resources, how they orchestrate our missions to obtain maximum effect. At the squadron level we rarely get to hear the brass talk openly about what they're doing, but in the Forms 'D' and in the intelligence briefings we get a lot more. Learning to be a good operational fighter pilot isn't just learning to wear your Spitfire like a glove and throw it around the sky like it was a part of you, it's also learning what we are trying to do. If you're interested, stay close to me; ask me questions; read the Forms 'D'; hang out at the Intelligence Officer's tent and pick up what's coming in on the teletype. It'll not only be interesting, but I feel certain it'll pay off. I have the feeling you're going to make one hell of a good fighter pilot."

And that's what Frank began to do.

He learned that in the past year the squadron flew four types of missions: (a) missions escorting heavy bombers of the US 8thAF — B-17 Flying Fortresses and B-24 Liberators to the German border and meeting them again on their way out, (b) missions where a few medium bombers escorted by many squadrons of fighters would bomb a German air base hoping to coax the Luftwaffe fighters into battle, (c) some escort missions for convoys of ships travelling through the Channel, and (d) occasional sweeps in which several squadrons of fighters 'swept' a broad area hoping to entice combat. However, in December 1943, Allied intelligence learned that a special German army organization responsible for launching the pilotless bomb had become operational with the intention of firing the first bomb in February. Soon after, reconnaissance flights reported sighting many compact facilities consisting of two main buildings, several nisson huts and a ski-shaped ramp appearing in many wooded areas in France and Belgium close to the coast. All were heavily defended.

Further intelligence indicated these were the pilotless bomb launch sites and 2ndTAF HQ singled them out as priority targets. So it was that since Christmas more and more missions were to escort medium bombers hitting pilotless bomb launch sites in northern France and Belgium. Allied intelligence had found out that Hitler promoted the development of several diabolical weapons — weapons he was convinced could win the war. They were called reprisal weapons, *Vergeltungswaffe*. The first model called the V-1, was a pilotless aircraft that consisted of a 1,870 pound bomb, propelled by a simple pulsing ramjet mounted above it. It was aimed and launched to a range set by the simple mechanism of a small propeller in the nose that cut the fuel supply at the proper distance. It was small, cheap to manufacture and when launched by the thousands could well have wreaked such havoc upon London as to destroy the English people's will to fight. Other German weapons were so secret no one knew what they could be, but each was described as being more horrific than its predecessor.

In the months ahead, the Allies learned of the terrifying V-2 rocket bomb that hit and exploded before it could even be seen let alone intercepted. And after the war, it was learned that the Germans were well along in their research into creating a battery of super-guns (the V-3 weapon) that could hit London. And all of this was in addition to the work being done in developing an atomic bomb. But none of this information was known at the time.

After escorting medium bombers to the V-1 sites, Spitfire pilots usually strafed the target area as on Ramrod 416 on 4 January when the de-briefing report stated that several nisson huts were set on fire by the strafing, but that the target was well bombed by the medium bombers to the point where all the newly-constructed structures construction were completely demolished. Apart from the flak Frank was getting to enjoy these missions. He longed to have a crack at an enemy aircraft, but if that wasn't to be, he could still get a kick out of these ground attacks.

On 5 January, the wing rendezvoused with Mitchells over Domfront, south of Caen and in the Normandy countryside. The Mitchells had been deep inside France and were a little late for the rendezvous. The point to pick up the escort was already close to the greatest distance from base that the Spitfires could penetrate. As they approached the Mitchells there where a half dozen Me 109s seen far below, about to attack. One Me 109 was caught by the fire from a Mitchell and was seen to go down in flames and crash. But as soon as the Spitfires appeared the other enemy pilots "dove for the deck to escape."[†] Conrad led Red Section after the Me 109s with Frank flying Red Four and anticipating his first kill. But they could not catch the enemy aircraft. The Spitfire escort returned home, but with the delay in rendezvous and the attempt to catch the enemy aircraft, every aircraft recorded hardly any fuel left in its tanks when it landed.

---

† 421 Squadron ORB 5 January 1944

Weather in the UK at this time of the year is usually pretty spotty, and the January of 1944 was no exception, with many days in which there was no flying at all. Almost all the missions were flown at wing-strength escorting the medium bombers — Bostons and Mitchells — of No.2 Group of 2ndTAF, although on some occasions they flew escort to the Marauders of the US 9thAF. V-1 launch sites were springing up like mushrooms near the coast in France and Belgium and as quickly as they were being destroyed others were coming into being. These sites were dubbed 'No-ball' sites since they were launching points for pilotless aircraft. Hitler instigated a massive build-up of these locations because, as Allied intelligence had just confirmed, he planned to launch thousands of these flying bombs every day in order to subdue Britain.

The 421 pilots were not extremely fond of these V-1 launch targets because they were always heavily defended by flak. However, the Spitfires were usually flying high cover that kept them relatively safe from the flak concentrations while the medium bombers went in at 7000 to 8000 feet — high enough to avoid light flak — and had to hold straight-and-level in their bomb run amidst a storm of exploding 88mm shells with proximity fuses. A few of the flak bursts reached the height of the Spitfires. While below the Marauder pilots flew on seemingly unaffected, above Frank felt the petrifying shock of the first blasts exploding around him. For an instant he froze and watched the first yellow-black explosion erupt a hundred yards to his right and below him. He could sense shrapnel hurtling towards his Spitfire, but as he held his breath, there was no jolting shudder of metal pieces tearing into the aircraft. Recovering quickly, he began weaving as were the other aircraft in the section. The performance of the Marauder pilots who flew on through the worst of the flak was an awesome display of steady nerve and staunch courage that the Spitfire pilots greatly admired. In a little over a month they were to learn that they would be called upon to do not only that courage-testing feat, but to better it.

*   *   *

IN ADDITION to gathering information about missions, Frank talked to the Engineering Officer about the current and future development of the Spitfire. He learned that as early as 1941 the Supermarine Company and the RAF were trying to do something about the limited range of the Spitfire. Designers of fighter aircraft had to consider the trade-off between the weight of fuel and the weight of armaments. Since the aircraft were small, the designers compromised to produce a maximum of firepower but at the cost of limiting fuel and hence providing short range. Spitfires used for reconnaissance missions could be stripped of armament and ammunition and augmented with additional wing and fuselage tanks, to give nearly twice the normal range — although distributing the fuel around like this made the pilot very aware of shifts in centre of gravity and required considerable skill in switching from one tank to another to keep the aircraft in flying trim. The Japanese demonstrated that external fuel tanks positioned close to the centre of gravity and jettisoned just before attack, were an excellent solution to the problem. Both sides in the conflict engaged in intense research to find the right size and shape of these extra fuel tanks.

Reginald Joseph Mitchell, designer of the Spitfire, had settled upon two internal fuel tanks, located right in front of the pilot at the centre of gravity of the airplane, totalling 87 gallons capacity. This happened to be much the same compromise that Willie Messerschmitt had settled upon when designing the Me 109. With a specific fuel consumption of about 0.8 gallons per hour for the Rolls-Royce Merlin engine and a full load of two 20mm cannon, four machine guns and maximum ammunition for all, the Spitfire Mk IX had a maximum operational flying time of about two hours. At full power, the conditions in which dogfights were conducted, consumption increased to 1.1 gallons per hour or more. Blend a normal take-off segment, flight to a combat zone, engagement in combat and a return segment, and this cut the operational time to an-hour-and-a-half or so. During the Battle of Britain, when the Germans were attacking across the Channel, taking a half-hour to cross the Channel and another half-hour to return, they could only spend 20 minutes over the UK. That was greatly to the advantage of the RAF who could fly all-out from take-off until their ammunition ran out. Now the situation was reversed: the RAF had to fly across the Channel to operate over Europe where the advantage moved to the defender and the challenge rose to the aggressor.

The answer was external fuel tanks of various sizes and configurations, and this became a great source of experimentation and sometimes, solution. But there were difficulties. So it is that on the mission of the 7 January 1944, there is the telling comment:

> "Six radiators damaged when 45-gallon tanks were jettisoned. Aircraft were in straight and level flight when tanks were dropped."

The 45-gallon teardrop tank was a new and not very successful experiment. Soon the standard would become the 45-gallon or 90-gallon slipper-tank that fit snugly under the aircraft fuselage blanketing the air intake.

*   *   *

ON 14 JANUARY, Ramrod 453 provided a moment of excitement when the wing spotted two FW 190s flying very low north of Amiens. They were about to attack, but the radio transmitter in W/C Godefroy's aircraft was malfunctioning, and being unable to convey instructions to his men, he called off further action. It was another disappointment for Frank who wished he could have gone to the attack.

In this period Frank flew a couple of Spitfires with the serial numbers MA794 or MK907. The latter seemed to be his favourite, and when he wasn't flying it, his roommate at Kenley, F/L Bill Stronach was. It was a good airplane. There were 28 pilots on the roster of 421 Squadron and only 18 aircraft allotted to them, so only the squadron commander, the two flight commanders and one or two senior pilots always flew the same aircraft day after day. They were the ones who painted the names of girl friends or images of comic strip characters on the cowlings and gave names to the aircraft. All the other pilots shared aircraft and with the 'every-second' mission sequencing, this usually meant two pilots shared a single aircraft flying it on alternate days. However, aircraft often got shot up or had to have periodic maintenance and overhaul and when this happened the pair of pilots would shift to another Spitfire. In January Frank also flew MA232 and BS200 for a few days until MA794 and MK907 were back from periodic maintenance.

There were large numbers of Allied aircraft entering the European airspace at all times during late January 1944. RAF Bomber Command sent heavy bombers every night into Germany where it hurt the most — Berlin and the deep Fatherland — while the US 8thAF pounded German cities throughout the day. To accompany this deep penetration of Nazi airspace during the day was the truly remarkable aircraft — the P-51 Mustang, that was found to be large enough to have the capacity to carry enough fuel to fly all the way to Berlin, and still have the vitality and manoeuvrability to fight off any German defender. Several factors altered the nature of the battle in the skies over Western Europe at this time. Because of the unrelenting pressure inflicted by the bombing inside Germany, Hitler withdrew all but two Luftwaffe fighter units from the west to the heartland of Germany. And to compensate, he doubled the strength of the flak units in France and the Low Countries and co-ordinated their action with radar, night fighters and search lights. RAF Bomber Command losses increased due to the increased flak concentration and deadly night-fighters while over Germany the US 8thAF encountered unacceptable loss rates until enough Mustang fighter groups were operational to protect the huge Flying Fortresses and Liberators. In the race for control — Germany to strengthen fighter defence at home and the US to strengthen bomber escort — the culmination came in the last weeks of February in what became known as 'Big Week' when an enormous victory was achieved. The USAAF claimed 305 enemy fighter aircraft destroyed between 10 February and 25 February with 90 of them claimed destroyed 10 and 11 February.

The Germans were desperate. They unleashed several last-minute aviation marvels including the jet-powered Me 262 and the rocket-powered Me 163. These very superior weapons were far too few in number to influence the results of the war. But the greatest threat was yet to come — Allied intelligence gathered more and more information about the dreaded 'Vengeance-weapons'— the

V-1 flying bomb and some sketchy information regarding a rocket and a super-gun.

In the month of January the squadron mounted operations on only 14 days for a total of 21 missions. Frank was now flying regularly for he flew eleven of these missions — six of them in the last week of January. The last of these was flown at 1530 hours 30 January. It was a fighter sweep through Belgium in the Brussels area. They spotted no enemy aircraft but at some locations the flak was pretty intense. This was the mission Frank referred to when he said, " ... I've formed a very healthy respect for the accuracy of German ack-ack — I almost had an enforced stay in Belgium the other day." That mild statement hid a massive feeling of fear that all pilots expressed whenever they referred to flak, but it revealed his growing confidence.

It was with great delight that the squadrons of 127 Wing saw the arrival of the first batch of new Mark IXb Spitfires. For over two years after it first appeared in 1941, the FW 190 had been the scourge of the RAF. It became known as 'the butcher bird'. The RAF had countered with the Spitfire Mark V that first appeared in late 1942. But although the Mark V could compete against the FW 190 at low altitude — its single compressor kicking in at 8000 feet — it was completely outclassed at anything higher. In the hands of a very capable pilot, an inferior aircraft could overcome a better aircraft, and so there were those who could handle the FW 190. But for most Allied pilots the FW 190 was just too good. It was in the Mark V that Frank learned to fly a Spitfire at Kirton-in-Lindsey. The answer to the FW 190 was a new version of the Spitfire — the Mark IX.

Figure 15 — F/L Johnny McElroy is seen here studiously painting the Indian head crest on the cowling of his new Spitfire. All 421 aircraft bore this emblem.

(McElroy collection)

Throughout 1943, 421 and 403 Squadrons flew the first version of the improved Spitfire Mark IXa. Now the two squadrons were receiving the further improved Mark IXb. Spitfire IXs had a more powerful engine, and a two-stage compressor — one stage kicked in at 8000 feet and the other at 12,000 feet. This made the Spitfire IX more than an equal — many would say, vastly superior — to the FW 190.

Spare time was quickly occupied by painting squadron Indian heads (421 Squadron had obtained the support of the McColl-Frontenac Oil Company whose emblem was an Indian head) and started to apply it to these new machines. More excitement flowed through the base at Kenley as 416 Squadron joined the wing at the beginning of February, bringing the wing to a total of three squadrons.

In early February Frank sent two letters to Bev:

"421 Squadron
RCAF England
2 February 1944

Dear old Joe,

I'm afraid I was a very poor correspondent during January — not to anyone in particular but to everyone in general. I've never written so few letters in a month since I left Canada. As you can imagine we had a fairly busy month. And I find that the more ops I do the more I feel I must get out bingeing at night and on duff days of doing anything but sitting placidly in the mess reading a book or writing letters. That's my excuse and a bloody poor one it is too when you stop to think, as it implies nothing more nor less than a lack of will-power. Ops aren't tiring in the strict sense of the word but rather they are exhilarating and just make a chap want to keep on at something reasonably active such as whipping down the hill to catch the London train, crashing around in the blackout from pub to pub, then staggering back to the station for a few hours sleep so you can do it all over again the next day. Actually, January for me was, far from being a month of over-work and exhaustion merely a month of following the line of least resistance and mild dissipation — as you so capably described (in one of the four letters I received from you during the last month) as a really 'spoiled life' that is going to be the crux of all our post-war rehabilitation problems. Yes sir Joe. I got four excellent and tremendously appreciated letters from you since I last wrote on 30 December. One, dated 30 December I received two weeks ago, and the other three, dated 16 January (a long letter requiring much answering), 20 January (with some very interesting clippings) and 21 January (an air letter), all three of which I received today. So actually, this rather diminutive form is more of an insult than a reply to your letters, but is meant merely to break the silence while I do the necessary amount of thinking to answer your letters properly. It is such a treat to receive and especially read your letters, Joe. They are not only newsy in a mild sort of way (and 'newsiness' in any stronger form is, I think, the greatest pitfall threatening any would-be letter writer) but more important, they are full of the thinking man that you are. When you are separated from someone of whose friendship is not merely professed but real, you are not essentially interested in hearing from him or her of the many little indecisive actions that go to make their day (except those that may leave a lasting enough impression on their mind to in some way change their way of thinking), but you are essentially interested in their process and products of thought. It doesn't interest me terribly to hear that you got gloriously squiffed on quantities of Mascatto, but it does interest me tremendously to hear, if, as a result of that orgy, you have a little council-of-war with yourself and decide to 'tea-total' for the rest of (what would then be) your miserable existence. So it is refreshing and damn good for me to pick up your letter out of the pile and sit down to a really enjoyable bit of reading. I'm glad we have been able to keep our letters on a sort of thinking plane, Joe, it all goes to help us keep on knowing each other so that no matter how often or long we're separated, we can still hello again without feeling self-conscious or doubtful. Seems I just started this bloody thing and here the end hovers in sight. I'm going to sacrifice speed for quality in my next letter and write an ordinary letter. These new-fangled speed-mad Airgraphs and such-like forms are OK as far as reminding a person that you are thinking of them, but for telling them how you are thinking of them and what you think of them (unless it's bad when a telegram is the safest missile) you can't beat an old-fashioned letter of 12 pages or so of thought and composition. And now, before closing, for the news — I've formed a very healthy respect for the accuracy of German ack-ack — I almost had an enforced stay in Belgium the other day.

Young Barry is walking now and joins with me in thanking his Godfather so very much for remembering him on his first birthday with a silver napkin ring which will remind him throughout his life of the respect, which he will learn to share, I know, which his father has for old Joe Baily. Let me remind you that this is just to sort of break the silence 'til I settle down to write the long letter that you deserve. Success to Temperance.

Frankie"

On the third of February Frank flew Ramrod 505. This time he flew Red 3 with F/O Packard his wingman, while F/L Sherlock flew S/L Conrad's wing man. It was another uneventful sweep of the area from Lille to Cambrai and on to Boulogne. Then three days later, Frank flew high cover for 72 B-26 Marauders of the US 9thAF bombing Courmeilles-sur-Vixion. Two Me 109s were sighted attacking a straggling Marauder. Frank's Blue section was detailed to attack them. They dove to the attack but the enemy disappeared into thick cloud and escaped before they could be found. Frank's section then escorted the straggler until he was well clear of the French coast. Once again Frank's wish to prove himself in combat had been foiled.

"Feb 5 1944

Dear old Joe,

Contrary to what I expected when I got up this morning, I don't think I'll have much work to do this morning so am now sitting by the fire in our Pilot's Intelligence Room and thought that this would be an ideal opportunity to at least make a start on this letter. It is still quite early in the morning (9 am) and as I sit here I can hear overhead the thundering roar of American bombers as they start out on their trip to France where our boys will meet them within the hour. It takes us about half the time that it takes them to get there so we won't be taking off for a while yet. Our job will be to keep any enemy fighters that may pop up to have a go, away from them so they can concentrate on their bombing. It looks as though it might be a bloody good do as there are lots of Hun fighters in the area that the bombers are passing through, and when I was awakened quite early this morning for briefing I was sure I'd be on the show. But the lineup was changed at the last minute so here I am sitting on my prat while the lucky 12 that are going are getting their kit on down at dispersal, checking their parachutes, giving their kites a last-minute check-over before zero hour, which is in about 30 minutes. In the Intelligence

Room here we have a radio receiver hooked up so that we can hear all the boys R/T chatter from the time they take off until they land. Sometimes it's quite interesting to listen to especially if they run into any Huns. So when they take off I'll switch the set on and if anything exciting happens I'll be able to write it down for your amusement. I was rather peeved to be awakened so early this morning and then to find I'm not on the show but I really can't kick as I've been on the last three and we have so many pilots in the squadron that if you average one do in three you're doing pretty well. Things will be different though when the Invasion does come through, as we were more or less told to expect about 40% casualties for the first little while until the Luftwaffe has had all the 'Luft' knocked out of it.

When I mentioned just a second ago that I was peeved at being awakened so early for my days work, it just struck me that there was a typical example of what you so ably described in your last letter as "the spoiled life" we are leading in the services. My golly, after the war I'll have to do my own waking up to get to work — that is, if I'm lucky enough to have any work to go to. I'm afraid, Joe, that all you said in that letter was much too true to warrant any contradiction or elaboration from me. Just at the time of our lives when we would normally have been coming in contact with the hardness of the world and the inconsistencies and discouragements of making a beginning in our life as individuals, here we've been tossed into the lap of luxury of a temporary but strictly ordered unindividualistic and effortless sort of life. In other words we are still going to have to meet the world as beginners when this war is over, but, instead of doing so as young men of 19 or 20 fresh from the idealisms and infinite possibilities of school life, we're going to do so as old-young men of 24 or 25 who have seen too much in too short a time, who have found the free and easy life of wartime pleasant, simple to live but hard to forget when faced with the much more difficult task of living a successful, peaceful life where passions and desires must be controlled and not given free reign as they are now. Many of us are going to be faced with the many problems of real married life too, which has never really presented themselves in the haphazard, exotically happy sort of married life a chap gets in wartime. All in all, Joe, I think both you and I think alike when we realize the difficulties that are going to be presented by taking off the old uniforms for good. Thank gosh the Joes are what they are. It'll make it easier for us all to be able to get together once in a while and bitch and plan in the same language.

You'll have to pardon my style of composition, Joe, (i.e. a one-paragraph letter). Blame it on the war and these blasted air letter forms that defy good composition. That incidentally, is just another example of how war makes a man lazy. Say, summing all of this chatter of ours up Joe, I suggest that, if you haven't already and if you can get it, you read Tolstoy's *War and Peace*. It is marvelously well written, very long and of the Napoleonic era. But war is war no matter what century it is in and it has the same basic effects upon man. If you can't get the book, Joe, let me know and I'll send you mine.

The boys took off sometime ago and we're just beginning to get transmissions from them now. Nothing of interest has happened so far but there are some Huns in the air and it looks as if the boys might run into them. There is quite a gang in the room here now so it's just a bit difficult to continue writing comprehensively. Oops! — got to fly so will have to continue this later.

When I said later I didn't think it would be this much later — Feb 7th 1944.

However, here it is Monday afternoon and as the weather is bad the wing has been released for the afternoon — so I should be able to sit down and finish this without interruption. Was kept busy all Saturday afternoon and I didn't have a chance to finish this then. Saturday night a bunch of us got together in the bar before dinner got pretty whistled and cracked off to a dance in Caterham — you probably remember the place as I think you used to be stationed right around this district. Got down there in time to complete the 'whistling process' before the bar closed and then slid (and I do mean it literally!) down stairs to have a go at the dance — what a bunch of bags! In the process of voicing our dislike of the stuff that was pushing around the dance floor we must have got a bit noisy, as we left shortly afterwards — at the manager's request. Yesterday we were out on a long show that took us right over Paris — could see the Eiffel Tower in all its glory. We were quite high and the temperature was minus 45C — I almost froze to death as my electrically heated jacket and gloves weren't working. Tore a wicked strip out of my wireless mechanic when I came back. Last night we went out boozing again to a little place I had been to once before — a girl I met at a dance had taken me there one night. The name will kill you — 'The Old Mid-Whitgiftian Club'. We got pretty stinko again, but our behaviour must have been a bit more refined, as the people there didn't even suggest tossing us out.

So I was rather thankful when I got up this morning to see low cloud, fog and rain. Spent the morning sleeping by the fire in our dispersal hut.

Got a letter from your Mom today which I certainly appreciate. Her description of your young nephew was killing — quote, "Hear from Bella that things at the house are as usual in an uproar. The kid hit Bella with the hair brush, nearly choked the cat to death, broke the handle of his new cart — next thing he'll be burning the joint down." That is what Frank had written in a letter to your Mom.

Also heard from Junie, but not much news. I'm sure I've told you before, but might as well tell you again — young Barry is walking. Junie is mailing you the latest pictures taken of him, so you'll be able to see him at the age of one.

Got quite a surprise Saturday night just before we left for the dance, when old Joe Wilson phoned me. He is at Gunnery School flying student gunners around and he is really brassed. I hadn't answered his last couple of letters so he just phoned to see what the hell was the matter with me. Laziness was my answer. He's going to try to get a couple of days off and come down and visit me here.

Think I mentioned in my last letter that Kenny was down here for a weekend. He's becoming quite a Romeo, Joe. But he still is a very careful and precise drinker. By golly he's changing though. We had bags of fun — went to a dance at the Overseas League in London and we cut a few capers.

"When the war is over and we go back home ...", was followed by some very true and vivid remarks in your letter. It's certainly not going to be easy to fit into our little niche of peacetime living after four or maybe more years in the services. For one reason, we left civilian life as boys — we shall go back to it boys in more ways than one and yet expected to take our place as men in a communal life of which we have no clear conception and for which we have no applicable training. We have one thing on our side though, Joe, besides our loved ones who will always be a source of inspiration and help to us, and that is a certain widening of our social consciousness — an increased tolerance — a broadening of our mind and understanding or whatever you want to call the actual philosophical or psychological process, which has been brought about, I think, by our four or more years of meeting a wide variety of types not only from all walks of life but also from many of the various nations in the world that were to us once nothing more than geographical shapes or colours on a map. Now I claim that this widening of our outlook, although it may have no immediate or tangible effect upon our conversion from soldier to civilian — such as helping you get a job, and once having one, help you keep it — or help you to always refer to the shit house as the toilet, or say "my goodness" instead of "fuck me" — will be invaluable in keeping us find happiness, interest and beauty in a life that might otherwise have been narrow and local. And after all, Joe, if you can find happiness and beauty and maintain an active interest in the life you are living, don't you think that at least half your purpose in life, has been accomplished?

I think our years in the service have developed our appreciation of happiness and have shown us that it is not hard to find if we look for it in simple, basic actions and realize the simplicity of a happy state of mind. I think we have learned a bit about where and how to find happiness as we have had to rely entirely on ourselves for that particular commodity, during most of our service life. And under those conditions, it's natural that a chap should discover how simple and easy it is to be happy.

I think our years in the service have helped to develop our sense of beauty, chiefly by presenting to our view different landscapes, skies, flowers, birds, trees, architecture that we have never seen before. And as it increases our discovery of beauty it increases our own appreciation of it. And then of course, in a life where so much ugliness, distortion and sordidness present themselves, we instinctively want beauty and need it and therefore look for it. And once you start honestly looking for beauty, it is not hard to find nor its discovery disappointing. I've noticed in you, Joe, since you left Canada an increased perception and appreciation of beauty. So I do think the service life helped us somewhat in this respect.

I think also, that our years in the service have more noticeably increased our interest in life. We have seen so many new countries, peoples, laws, currencies, vehicles, customs, foods, drinks, entertainments etc. which would have been of abstract interest in a normal peacetime existence but which are of vital and real interest to us now because we have seen them. What was before the war our local and almost entirely communal interest in life, has now become an international interest in the world which is our life. The more you have to interest you, the less time you have to be despondent or feel life to be dull and empty.

I hope I haven't been too vague and dogmatic in my support to your views on our post war difficulties of adjustment. The war has definitely made things harder for us to start off our struggle with life, but I think it has also given us something that will make the job a little easier.

Well, I've certainly dragged this letter out to some length. Rather longer and more serious than I had intended. But your letters always stimulate thought in me, and the best way to crystallize your thoughts into comprehensible units is to try and write them down — they sometimes even become clear to yourself then!

Well, it's just about time I got cleaned up and changed for dinner. As far as I know there's nothing on the agenda for tonight except the usual starting session in the bar, and then I rather imagine a letter to Junie followed by a bath and bed.

Sorry to hear that recreational facilities are somewhat limited where you are now, Joe. Can only suggest that you do a little descriptive writing for your own amusement.

I'll write again soon and in the meantime look after yourself.
Success to temperance.
Frankie"

Frank was once again on a mission 9 February, on Ramrod 537. He flew with his friend Charlie Grant and Johnny Sherlock in Blue Section. The wing swept Abbeville, Merville, Arras and Amiens. The visibility was poor but they vectored into reported enemy aircraft only to find none there. During the middle of February F/L Karl Linton and F/L Ed Gimbel took turns leading the squadron as Wally Conrad was sidelined with a severe cold.

Before the month was over, Frank wrote once again upon this troubling issue of how he and Bev would fare when they had to tackle a civilian life that neither of them knew:

David W Clark

"421 Squadron
RCAF England
Feb 27, 1944

Dear old Joe,

Haven't written for a couple of weeks, so figure it's about time I let you know that I'm still alive and kicking and bloody glad to hear from you again. Have received two letters from you since I last wrote, one dated February second which enclosed some very interesting clippings and an old one dated December seventh enclosing a Frontenac White Cap Ale label — you old bastard. Would most certainly have answered them sooner except that I have been very busy both days and nights since my last letter on February 7. We've been doing a lot of ops this month as the weather has been pretty decent. A lot of the shows have been done from advanced bases near the coast too, and have been stranded at such places several times from bad weather or unserviceable aircraft, so it has been a pretty active month for me as ops go, and I haven't had any leave since Kenny visited me in January. So day letter-writing has been pretty well out. On duff days I generally trotted up to London for drinking sessions or played cards here. And as for the nights — I've done quite a bit of tearing about this month, but have stopped for awhile now — I'm broke.

Wish you could have come to spend a few days with me here at the squadron before you left as it is one of the most 'drinkingest' messes I've ever been in and really has a shit-hot bar.

The other night I was in the bar drinking with a few of the boys and they ran out of scotch. So we switched to gin until that ran out and then we were really stumped until one of the fellows noticed a bunch of pretty looking different shaped bottles behind the bar, which on investigation turned out to be various kinds of liqueurs plus a couple bottles of fancy wines and one of Hoc. So we settled down again on our stools, got the barman to line them up on the bar and proceeded to finish a bottle of crème-de-menthe, ambroisette, Austrian Maraschins, Ginger Brandy, the two bottles of wine and the one of Hoc. It must have been a good drunk — it sure cost us enough. Parts of it though, especially towards the end, are pretty hazy in retrospect. I couldn't move till noon the next day. And that is just one of the several nights that have eaten up the old bank roll this month. I have however, done a few useful things with my money. I saw the film *For Whom the Bell Tolls* and the *Lisbon Story* — both of which

88

made very decent entertainment and I sent Junie some flowers for Valentine's Day, which I trust further endeared me to my dear wife.

Golly Joe, where I am now is just a lovely spot for pitching parties and drunks and other escapades — if only you were here it would be wonderful. What fun we could have! Actually I am stationed very near to where you were stationed yourself when I had lunch at your camp that day. How's the set-up down where you are? I guess the Eyties aren't really any too friendly are they? And I can't say I'd go for the mud and rain and muck that the newspapers say is breakfast, lunch and dinner for you fellows down there. The trouble is you know, Joe, this air force life is absolutely spoiling me in almost every respect except that it has broadened my mind in a few things such as authority, responsibility, good types and bad types and has given me a bit more patience. Otherwise it has made me lazy, taken away my initiative and ambition, almost destroyed my idealism and given me a very gloomy concept of the mentality of mankind. As you probably are guessing, I think this damn war has gone on long enough and I shall be quite glad to see the end of it. Although the life I'm leading right now is probably one of the easiest and luxurious and, at times enjoyable, I shall ever have the opportunity of leading again — it is also the most pointless and purposeless. No matter how hard a life might be, how arduous the work and how little the play, if it is towards a goal or for a purpose, it is I think quite happy — a balanced type of happiness I mean. Not the ecstatic kind of happiness or super-joy brought on by a bottle of whiskey which flames and dies like the setting sun — only to be followed by the painful darkness of a horrible hang-over.

So although I really do enjoy the carefree, gay, mad parts of this sort of life you and I are living — underneath it all runs a steady current of dislike which only asserts itself at moments like this when I sit down and really try to get my thoughts into some sort of comprehensive design. And that undercurrent will continue to persist, and in you too I think Joe — because we are really by temperament carefree enough to thoroughly enjoy and feel at home a carefree, haphazard fly-by-night sort of life. We think a bit too seriously and curiously about life — which is, I think, a good thing and is more likely to get us that balanced sort of happiness when we can finally settle down again and live normal sort of lives.

I seem to remember painting a rather different picture of the effects of a service career on the normal chap, in my last letter which you are probably just about to hold up in a protest to my last few remarks. The two different points of view can only mean two things (1) either there is a bit of good in every evil (or conversely there is a bit of evil in all that's good) or (2) that I'm still immature enough that I still don't know my own mind and merely shoot off my mouth on such matters to impress people. Upon retrospect, I'm inclined to take the last meaning as being nearer the truth.

So having made a point, supported it with a few arguments and then immediately ridiculed both the point and the arguments — it doesn't leave much for you to enlarge on in your next letter except to say what you are probably thinking right now — "The silly bastard."

We were very fortunate here in having with us for a few days a Captain Gus Day, a Canadian infantry officer who had been all through the Sicilian campaign and through the Italian show as far as Campobasso. He gave us a very interesting lecture so I now have a better idea of what you are doing in Italy and under what conditions. He could of course tell us more of the details than you could in your letters and some of them really opened my eyes. I think I'll bust off to tea for the moment and finish this after ....

Dear old Joe — Ooops! — I left you to have some tea — Well —- I had my tea — then several beers then I had dinner — then I had the old liqueur deal I mentioned earlier in this letter with five other fellows with the result that I'm not exactly sober right now as you can probably tell by the writing — that is, if you can read it. Anyway Joe, old cock, I had just about written myself out by the time I went over for tea — and what better way to end a letter to one's best pal than by being gloriously drunk — success to temperance —- and for God's sake take care of yourself Bev.

Frankie"

   As with January there were many days in February when 421 Squadron did no flying at all. A total of 24 operational missions were carried out in 18 days of flying in February. Frank flew 12 of the missions; exactly half.

Chapter Six

F OR THE fighter wings of 2ndTAF, two new roles were added to that of aerial interdiction to turn the fighter into a ground support weapon. They fitted Spitfires with bomb racks to hold a 500-pound bomb under the fuselage or two 250-pound bombs under the wings to turn them into dive-bombers. And in addition to the dive-bombing role, a ground strafing attack role was added. These two roles required special training. Each of the three squadrons spent a week in March at No.16 Hutton Cranswick Armament Practise Camp near the city of York, learning the technique of dive-bombing and gaining experience in air-to-ground firing. 421 Squadron's turn at this base was 2 March through 8 March, while 416 Squadron and 403 Squadron took the course together 9 March through 14 March

The dive-bombing technique taught the pilots consisted of approaching the target at 6,000 feet altitude, covering the target with the starboard wing tip, peeling off and diving at the target at a 60-degree angle, all the while holding airspeed to no more than 380 mph. At exactly 3,000 feet the bomb was to be released just at the start of the pull-out. This was an almost impossible task to perform because the Spitfire was very light, gained speed rapidly due to the efficiency of the wing design and had no dive brakes. It gained speed mercilessly in the dive and could not be held below 380 mph. Furthermore it was extremely difficult to know whether the aircraft was at 60-degrees or not, and with the altimeter unwinding like a fast clock it was difficult to pull out exactly at the intended 3,000-foot level. Nevertheless, some of the pilots, including Frank, learned the knack and performed well in the exercises. In Frank's letters home he often mentioned how much he enjoyed the ground attack role — diving at a steep angle lined up on a ground target, feeling the sudden jolt as the cannon and machine guns seemed to stop the Spitfire in mid air, watching the tracers and cannon shells speed ahead, slowing down like glowing ping pong balls until some hits were seen and then pulling out of the dive as the altimeter wound down to several hundred feet. The diving procedure was much the same for dive-bombing or ground attack, but there was one big difference. For ground attack the aircraft usually formed up line abreast — four aircraft blasting away at a train or a motor convoy stretched out across their line of vision. But for dive-bombing the aircraft (usually six carrying the bombs while the other six flew cover) attacked line astern — one after another because the target was concentrated. When it was the sixth aircraft's turn to come up over the target and dive in this proscribed form, it took one huge amount of courage and it involved actively combating one's terror knowing that the German anti-aircraft gunners, correcting on all prior dives, now had the range and trajectory for the next shots to be accurate. The pilots thought back to the days when they marvelled at the nerve of the Boston and Marauder bombers flying unswervingly into the flak clouds and realized that this was much worse. In the three months ahead, Frank flew on a great many of the squadron's dive-bombing and ground attack missions. He often led a section on these occasions, but he never lost that feeling of panic when he was about to dive into the expected flak.

Through his letters we can see how, since coming overseas, Frank grew much closer to Bev than ever before. Instead of buddies, they had become firm fast friends. And in the next letter he tells Bev about digging out the stack of letters he had received and about the satisfaction it gave him to re-read the many words that passed between them. Never completely out of his thoughts was the concern he felt about starting life again in the post-war milieu, but he adds a new thought — how will our wives be affected?

"Tuesday 21 March 1944
421 Squadron
RCAF England

Dear old Joe

It has been a pretty dull day, we haven't flown at all and so I spent the afternoon doing a bit of house cleaning — right in the proper spirit too as today is the first day of spring. We expect to move any time now and as we will be living in tents and only allowed 60 lbs of personal luggage, it means quite an extensive weeding out of kit and personal belongings to decide what stays and what goes with me. Well, during the course of this very interesting pastime (it reminded me of being let loose in my grandma's attic, where all her junk had accumulated over a period of years, as a small boy) I sorted out all my letters, packed 'em in a box and intend to send them home for safekeeping. And before I packed 'em up, I read through once again, all your letters — and had a hell of a good time. The times we have been together in the last nine months lived again just as vividly as retrospect can be. Each letter had some memorable occasion referred to, and contained some intangible characteristic as distinctively B D Baily as the old polka dot ties of school days. Strange how an ordinary letter can be so much the life blood of its author.

Well, I got such a kick out of re-reading those letters that I decided I'd better sit down and dash off a few words to you although I have really nothing to say. I've been exercising pretty rigourously the last few days and am consequently rather tired tonight and contemplating an early retirement — all of which is by explaining that I'm not in a very active mental state at the moment so will confine myself to thoughts and scribblings requiring a minimum of effort.

Which, incidentally, brings out something that I have been thinking of quite seriously of late. There is not doubt about it, Joe, that my mind, and I daresay this applies to thousands of young men in the services, has been pretty dulled and thickened by the last four years of service life. It has not had to contend with the weighty problems of school life or worry about the complex confusion of young manhood — because I have been sheltered like a hermit in his cave, from the normal ups and downs of life by the ordered 'right-or-wrong' dictum of a provided-for life. In other words simply this — the well-oiled mental machinery of school days has become rusty. Now it strikes me that before you can expect to step out of uniform into your life's job, or the beginning of same, and step successfully, not only must you be pretty sharp mentally but also you must have a pretty fair understanding of the general situation that you're stepping into i.e. post-war Canada with its possibilities and dead ends plainly in view.

So, with all the last 30 ponderous lines (at least I can still count) as introduction — here is my point — we're not going to be too mentally alert (to a peace-time set up, I mean) and we will have lost partial, if not complete touch with Canadian affairs — domestic, political and economic — so, why not take advantage of the Government's recent legislative go to college for a year or two; sharpen the old grey matter up somewhat; have a good lengthy look at the Canadian post-war panorama and decide just where we fit in. Now, not only does the government pay for your tuition and books, give you and your wife and child if any a living allowance for as long as your chosen course of study takes, but it is to be hoped that some of your friends will be doing the same thing in all probability at the same university, so you are sure of having your friends at hand for at least a year or so after the war to help you (reciprocally) to break out of your 'service-life-complex' shell into the sunshine of a peaceful citizenship.

It would be a healthy life, by which its lack of luxury would allow you to put to good advantage the importance of, and happiness to be found in basic elements of life that I'm sure three or four years in the services teaches every man.

The only real objection to it all, as far as I can see, lies with your wife. She (and I'm including Mary as your wife-to-be) feels the war as much, if not more than the man does because it entails separation from him which to a woman is an awful lot. She may balk at the idea of her husband more or less laying aside his and her social standing, after their reunion, by becoming a student again. She may even allow his necessary hours of study to become the equivalent of another separation. I say all that is possible, but if a chap loves his wife and knows his wife and she returns his love, it should be an easy thing together living students' lives for a year or so. It would certainly bring you closer together I think. And what is more progressive than a young married couple who can live and study together, both planning the life work that the husband is to enter and which will in return provide for them both. It would be life in all simplicity for a couple of years, but it would certainly cushion that shock of becoming a civilian with definite responsibilities and obligations overnight.

Those are just my points for it, of course. I'm not as yet convinced that going to college for a year or so is the form. I'm just thinking about it — what do you think?

Above all, I think it's about time we start passing some real honest-to-goodness post-war legislation in our own minds. It's not only planning our own future security but it's a privilege that our democratic way of life affords us and therefore shouldn't be abused. Up 'til now, I've practised procrastination whenever the future looms up in my mind — but I think it's about time to get cracking in earnest don't you?

Had a letter from Junie today in which she described in detail a weekend (March 4-5) she had spent up north at Val Morin with Cyn Tindall, Joan Postans and Marian (Beer) Gall. I don't mind saying it made me be pretty envious. On the other hand though, the people back home must be pretty envious at our opportunities of seeing how the other half of the world lives. Just yesterday, in all the glory of a perfect spring day, I saw Paris from 8000 feet. And although your present location doesn't sound much for anyone to be envious of, at least you've seen the Med and Gibraltar and oranges growing on trees and Italian operas in Italian Opera Houses.

We've lost four of our chaps since I last wrote you. It's strange how unimportant death seems in wartime — or rather, it's strange how calloused a man's appreciation of death can become just because death happens to be the most likely result of war. If one man dies it is a calamity — when 20,000 men die it is an incident.

Pretty soon you'll be reading of the Western Front in much the same way as we here are now reading of the Italian front. When that day comes, Joe, we'll be on the last lap of this bloody great waste of time, I hope. If the campaign against the Jap bastards should be made up only of volunteers, will you volunteer, Joe? I hardly think I shall, unless of course it's a case of — "Clark, you are appointed to volunteer for service in Japan." — when of course you might just as well be a hero and volunteer. I'm really anxious to get home though as soon as I can. A young married couple shouldn't be separated for too long, I don't think. They should grow up and mature as much as possible together, besides which, I think it's about time that young Barry had a sister!

By the Christ, Joe, I wish we could get together for one big binge before things start to pop over here. You'd best start pushing your boys right up through Italy and I'll meet you somewhere in Germany about next August or September — then what a party we'll have — wieners, sauerkraut and bags of beer and frauleins. By golly, you know, that's not beyond the realms of possibility either.

Watch your step in the meantime, Joe. I hear the Germans they've got in Italy are pretty tough scrappers. Remember the old "Morire est pro patria"— well it's much more sensible when it goes like this "Vivere est pro patria" — and in closing, "Successum est ad temperancium"

Frankie."

The four pilots who were lost that Frank referred to in his letter were from 403 Squadron. In early March, while 421 Squadron was taking the bombing and gunnery course, F/O James Hamilton Ballantyne of 403 Squadron was hit by flak while attacking ground targets after a Ramrod escort mission. He was unable to get out of his aircraft, crashed and was killed. That same mission — a sweep of the Evreux area in Normandy after the medium bombers were through, saw F/L David Goldberg shot down and captured as a prisoner of war. And as March came to an end, there were two non-combat deaths — F/O Richard Wright Dennison was killed in a flying accident due to engine failure while training and F/L Clifford George Pennock was killed while practising dive-bombing. Although there was much intermingling while crowded around the bar at the Officer's Mess at night, the squadron pilots stuck pretty much together, and so it is unlikely that Frank knew any of these 403 pilots well — perhaps not at all.

*   *   *

WHEN THE invasion of Europe was launched, 2ndTAF's job was to support the army. It was to do this job better that the bombing and strafing roles were added. When they were not patrolling the battlefield to ensure no enemy aircraft attacked supply lines, they were expected to bomb and strafe targets that the army specified. After all three squadrons completed their training, they participated in a series of large army assault exercises simulating the invasion. For the first four days of April amid such miserable weather conditions that the aerial part of the exercise was cancelled again and again, the army learned a great deal but because of weather the air force learned practically nothing at all. This was not a very good start. However, the bombing and gunnery training at Hutton Cranswick paid off. A week after the close of the army exercises on Ramrod 709, 403 Squadron flew eight aircraft carrying 500-pound bombs and supported by four more Spitfires flying top cover, successfully bombed the 'No-ball' V-1 launch site at Bouillencourt. It was the first time Spitfires had been used to dive-bomb an enemy target in Europe — and the results were reported as being very successful. Notwithstanding the success of this mission, and the intent to broaden the wing's mandate, the overall role of 127 Wing changed only slightly and very gradually over the next two months as they still flew more escort missions and more sweeps than dive-bombing missions.

It was many months later that the pilots in the squadrons learned what the big brass really thought about using the Spitfire as a dive-bomber and the Typhoon as a rocket launching weapon. In a Secret report prepared by the Operations Research Section of the Allied Expeditionary Air Force entitled *Accuracy of Attacks on Small Targets by Fighter-bombers and RP Fighters*, dated April 1944, it states:

> "During April a number of fighter-bombers and RP attacks were carried out on targets in France. The primary purpose of these operations was to give the pilots practice. At the same time it was hoped to obtain some index of the accuracy of bombing and RP shooting, for which purpose as much photo-recce as possible was carried out, including sending Mustang aircraft with the attacking aircraft in order to circle the target during the attack and so obtain strike photographs.
>
> The results however were disappointing:

Target Damage	Attack	Aircraft	Sorties per Hit
Mixed Bridges	dive-bombing	Spitfire (1 bomb)	180 - 90
		Typhoon (2 bombs)	90 - 45
	RP	Typhoon	3.5 - 2
Gun Positions	RP	Typhoon	6

> NOTE: Figures for attack on well defended targets may be very different from these, which are themselves disappointing."

The report went on to say that some pilots had learned to do much better than this but that even with a great deal of training it was unlikely that the accuracy could be such as to support the

Figure 16 — Andy MacKenzie is flung in the pool by F/L Johnny McElroy and F/L Frank Clark. Enjoying the spectacle are F/L Len Thorne, F/O Bill Cook and F/L Bill Stronach.

(McElroy collection)

army in dealing with small concentrated targets like machine gun positions. In the Second World War, the army never quite forgave the Air Force for not being a replacement for artillery.

This period was memorable to Frank for another reason — his idol, Andy MacKenzie got married 25 March. It was arranged that the whole squadron would go to Tunbridge to be there for the wedding. The adjutant, F/O Lloyd Hennessey, wrote the entries in the squadron ORB. His dour humour and matter-of-factness jump out in the entry for 25 March 1944:

"Flying Officer 'Andy' MacKenzie's big day dawned bright and clear (ground fog), squadron took off on practise dive-bombing at 0800 hours, but due to ground haze had to make low level attacks. One hood came off and landed on Caterham Hospital with no casualties. The bus left at 1215 hours for the MacKenzie-Jacks nuptials, and although the groom arrived a trifle late, the fatal words were pronounced at 1332 hours. The party commenced at Milden Manor, Tunbridge. A meal was served followed by many drinks and much kissing of the bride. As time wore on the party became somewhat rougher. When this witness staggered for home, the groom had just been thrown into the swimming pool. Evidently from there on everyone went swimming and it is hoped that no 'Red Indians' will be found incumbent at the bottom of the pool tomorrow morning. Here's many years of health, wealth and happiness to 'Andy' and 'Joyce'."

Nearly everyone in the squadron attended. They formed a procession, marching through town with Lloyd Hennessey holding a large bell while Frank Clark struck it in a kind of funeral dirge, thus mourning the death of Andy's bachelorhood. This march and much of the wedding and subsequent dunking episode was captured on Johnny McElroy's camera. As seen in the photo, two cigarette-smoking pilots threw Andy MacKenzie in the pool — Frank Clark and Johnny McElroy.

*   *   *

ALL LEAVE was cancelled 5 April 1944; the need for security surrounding the impending invasion turned the whole of southern England into a sealed, armed camp. One of the unbelievably fortunate facts surrounding the D-Day invasion was that although there were many over-flights by enemy aircraft during this period, apparently the German pilots' reports of the endless rows of war material were interpreted by the German High Command as a much larger army than was really there. The build-up for D-Day was underway with a million men, and hundreds of thousands of planes, tanks, trucks, guns, and packing crates stacked in every field and lined beside every road from Dover to Plymouth. But when the actual invasion came with only seven divisions in the assault force, building up to 30 divisions within a month, the German High Command was still convinced a force of another 20 divisions was waiting to cross the Channel at the Pas de Calais. This belief was insistently maintained until the middle of July.

Figure 17 — 421 pilots sitting in readiness in front of the dispersal hut at RAF Station Kenley in early April 1944. They are: F/L Ed Gimbel, F/L Johnny Drope, unrecognized, F/L Wally Quint, F/O Bob Murray, F/L Frank Clark and F/L Bill Stronach.

(McElroy collection)

In the midst of the sealing off of all southern England, 127 Wing was ordered to move from RAF Station Kenley close to London, to RAF Station Tangmere close to the south coast, 14 April. This was not only a move to a more convenient location to start the Normandy Campaign, it also represented another opportunity to test out the newly learned skills of packing up the whole base and moving to a new locale. But when the time came to move, terrible weather descended hampering the road convoys and holding the aircraft on the ground. The 127 Wing ORB tells the official story of the move as follows:

"April 13 —A conference of all section commanders of 127 Airfield was held and final arrangements were explained. Convoy commanders and leaders were appointed and the route was outlined. The CO stressed the importance of convoy discipline and emphasized how imperative it was that all billets and buildings occupied by 127 Airfield at Kenley be left in a tidy and clean condition. To attain this aim an officer and party will be left behind to carry out a final inspection, turn the buildings over, and check inventories with the Clerk of Works, Kenley. S/L Nash was detailed to proceed to Tangmere and arrange a new site for his personnel as the location previously selected is not now available for this section.

"April 14 — The Advance Party departed for our new location, RAF Tangmere, at 0900 hours and arrived on schedule at 1330. Under the command of F/L Cannon, Signals Officer, the party immediately began to get the camp organized. It started to rain heavily about 1700 hours, and everyone got drenched. Nevertheless, the site was ready by darkness for the main party's arrival on the 15 April. No operations were carried out at the base owing to inclement weather. Packing of main party's equipment and kit was completed.

"April 15 — The main party consisting of 120 vehicles, departed Kenley at 0900 hours and arrived on schedule at 1330. No insurmountable difficulties occurred on route. By 1700 hours all telephones were connected and electric light organized throughout the whole camp. By darkness all sections were organized for business and most personnel turned in early to recuperate from a very busy and tiring day. Owing to bad weather, the three Airfield squadrons were unable to proceed and remained at Kenley overnight. No operations were carried out but flying training was effected.

"April 16 — The camp awoke to find the rain coming down in torrents. That lasted all day, and out came the rubber boots and rain coats. Mud in great quantities began to appear. Fortunately, most sections of the Airfield were situated on high ground and the water ran off. Few tents leaked, though G/C MacBrien, OC 17 Wing, appeared to have got a bad one. This was quickly changed. Notification was received that W/C Hugh Godefroy (DSO, just acquired) DFC, was grounded for a rest. W/C Lloyd Chadburn DSO, DFC, was appointed as W/C Godefroy's successor. Owing to the very bad weather, no operations were carried out. For the same reason the aircraft were unable to fly into Tangmere."

The details of what happened, was a bit more colourful and perhaps more predictable. Fully expecting to fly out of Kenley right up until 14 April, the pilots planned a bang-up send-off party for that night. During the day, the pilots of 416 and 421 Squadrons flew only one mission — an escort mission to Namur — before arriving back at Kenley in heavy rain. The rain became a monsoon-like downpour. It rained, blew and socked in with periods of intense fog for the full four-day period between 14 April and 17 April. The pilots were on short-order call to vacate as soon as they could get their aircraft off the ground, but with nothing to do but wait, the Canadian pilots did what they were noted for — partied almost all day for the four days.

Many years later, one of the pilots, Bill Stronach, described how by the second day the partying was getting rougher and they pulled the old trick of putting black shoe polish on the soles of one of their number, hoisting him upside down on the shoulders of a group of pilots while the performer carefully placed footprints across the ceiling, all the while singing one of the multi-verse drinking songs everyone knew so well. After several hours and a following day of this traffic, the ceiling looked like a farmer's field after a stampede of elephants had passed through. S/L Conrad tried to reduce the destruction with a dinner in London on the second day, but they were no sooner back at the base when the partying resumed. By the third day, bored with footprints on the ceiling, they decided to add some more spice and drew straws to select the unfortunate fellow who would pull down his drawers and have his rear portions blackened.

Accompanied by much merriment this pilot (to this day no one has divulged exactly who he was) was hoisted high enough to implant this new image squarely on a main wall. Then a promising artist embellished the image by adding the necessary genitalia to complete the anatomy lesson. In the midst of roaring laughter a shouting pilot announced that several WAAFs were entering the Officer's Mess. While two officers delayed the entry of the WAAFs for a moment, several others rushed around for material and hung the massive portrait of the King and Queen (found in every Officer's Mess) over the offending image.

It is not recorded what the WAAFs said when they saw the ceiling, but it is known that the base commander immediately placed all of the squadron commanders of 127 Wing under house arrest. The day of this rowdiness was the day when W/C Lloyd Chadburn arrived to assume command of the wing. He had just recently been announced as the replacement for W/C Hugh Godefroy — the Wing Commander (Flying) — whose tour was time-expired. The base commander at Kenley called the three squadron commanders — Bob Buckham of 403 Squadron, Freddie Green of 416 Squadron and Wally Conrad of 421 Squadron — to a meeting where he told them he was going to court-martial all three with the most severe charges he could lay. Lloyd Chadburn is reported to have joined the meeting at this time and told the base commander that he would have to be court-martialed as well for he was there with the other men. After much sputtering and acclamations of repentance, the agreed solution to the problem was a heavy fine, sufficient to completely redecorate the Officer's Mess. The pilots of 127 Wing always thereafter insisted that as a result of the huge reparations levy placed on them by the base commander, the Kenley Mess became the best appointed Mess in the whole UK.

*   *   *

THE WING finally moved out of Kenley and was established in the fields surrounding RAF Station Tangmere where a town of tents was erected and pilots furnished with bicycles so they could ride to their dispersal huts near the main runways. Throughout the month, the British and Canadian troops practised seaborne landings in the bays across southern England; the British 50th Division trained in Operation Smash at Studland Bay near Bournemouth, while the 7th and 8th Brigades of the Canadian 3rd Division trained at Start Bay in Cornwall. The navy provided craft to transport the assault troops and provided fire support while the air force provided air protection during the landings. Although 421 Squadron participated in these operations, Frank didn't fly on any of the them.

There was another memorable event that happened at the end of April. Although W/C Godefroy was actually replaced by W/C Chadburn 14 April, his going-away party was planned for the end of the month. It was held at the Unicorn Pub in Chichester — the favourite watering hole for all the pilots at Tangmere and the six satellite airfields that surrounded it. It was a big formal party with A/M Harry Broadhurst, G/C Bill MacBrien, W/C Johnnie Johnson, W/C Mannifrank Brown and others making long speeches. The pilots guzzled their beer in complete boredom as late afternoon droned on into evening. Finally they drifted out in ones and twos and returned to base where a crap game was started in the 50-man Officer's Mess tent. Later, G/C MacBrien joined the group when the crap game was in high gear. He didn't play craps but liked to bet on the side, and he hated to lose. Ever since January there had been something brewing between G/C Bill MacBrien and F/L Ed Gimbel — no one was certain what it was. Ed Gimbel became acting-squadron commander when Jimmy Lambert was killed and he filled in again in January when Wally Conrad was sick. The friction between MacBrien and Gimbel likely arose in that period.

At one point in the crap game MacBrien grabbed up the bills for a side bet saying he won.

Gimbel shouted out, "You weren't *for* making the point, you bet *against* making the point."

MacBrien replied, "You're crazy."

At this point Gimbel stormed out of the tent. Everyone thought he was going to bed because he was pretty far gone. But minutes later Gimbel came back and stood outside the tent brandishing two handguns. He fired a bevy of shots, two of which went through the tent wall. One hit F/L Bill Stronach in the shoulder and completely spun him around while the other creased the crotch of Johnny McElroy's trousers — whereupon McElroy shouted "I've been neutered!"[†]

Hart Finley of 403 Squadron ran out of the tent and decked Gimbel and the party was over. Gimbel was confined to quarters pending court martial for 'endangering the lives of fellow officers' and immediately busted from F/L to F/O. The trial was eventually held 3 June 1944 but since no one would testify against Gimbel and MacBrien made sure no one knew he was there, the charges were dropped and it was agreed that F/O Ed Gimbel, DFC, would voluntarily resign from the RCAF and join the USAAF.

*   *   *

THE MONTH of April was notable for another important development — the implementation of the 'Transportation Plan'. The Allied military invasion planners contended from the outset that the French rail system and the radar communication system must be destroyed before a landing could be made in Normandy. Normandy is enclosed by the Seine and Loire rivers. If all the bridges across these two rivers were destroyed, rail and truck transport to the Normandy area would be cut off from Paris and northern France and thus it would be extremely difficult for the German Army to reinforce the Normandy garrison. The bridges were set as the first priority. The second priority was radar. All of the northern radar centres had to be destroyed if the invasion was to succeed. The third priority was marshalling yards. There were several key marshalling yards — like the one at Mézidon east of Caen — that handled enormous quantities of rail freight servicing the principal cities and towns of Normandy. Destroy these three elements — bridges, radar centres and marshalling yards — and the success potential of the landing in France would be greatly improved. The Transportation Plan was not well known because of the security factors and the fear that

† McElroy was not injured but many years later, when this episode was described in the author's web site, a woman contacted the author pointing out that McElroy was not neutered for he sired four daughters. The contact became the source of all those photographs noted to be 'McElroy Collection'.

hundreds of French citizens would become victims as a result of its implementation.

Prime Minister Churchill and the British Government insisted this plan would result in too many French and Belgian civilian deaths and must be abandoned. It took the personal intervention of President Roosevelt to prevail so that at the end of March, Overlord planners set out the objectives. In a Secret document dated 28 April[†] they identified 24 coastal defence installations and 28 railway centres — 10 as top priority, 9 as second and 9 as third. Between this date and victory in Normandy in August, these rail centres were hammered by heavy bombers, photographed, hammered again by medium bombers and hammered again. In addition, over 30 bridges across the Seine and Loire Rivers were targeted. Although criticism of the plan was rife because of the threat to the civilian population, actual casualties in the event were half those predicted while the French rail system was reduced to 20% of its pre-Transportation Plan capacity.

In the month of April, the wing flew 53 missions. 421 Squadron flew 18 of these and Frank flew six of them — all uneventful.

---

† Appendix 'B' to DHH 73/829 Day Fighter Narrative — April 1944.

Chapter Seven

MAY SAW an enormous increase in activity with the wing flying 121 missions — more than twice the April figure. 421 Squadron flew 42 of them and Frank was on 22 of these. That placed him in the group of a dozen pilots who flew most often. Three pilots — the squadron commander and two flight commanders — flew nearly every mission; a dozen flew over half the missions; the remaining dozen flew one in every three or four missions.

On the first of May, Frank flew Red 2, wing man to Johnny McElroy when they swept the area around Juvincourt near Reims and shot up ten or more barges near St Quentin. Softening up the whole Western European sector was setting the stage for invasion, although target selection was a little tricky because the Allies had to fly more missions to the Pas de Calais area, so as not to tip their hand that Normandy was the planned landing site. The operations became considerably more complex.

Consider Ramrod 822 and Ramrod 831. On the second of May, Ramrod 822 consisted of three almost simultaneous attacks — 72 B-26 Marauders of US 9thAF attacking the railway centre at Busigny, a small town 50 miles (80 kilometres) east of Amiens, others attacking the marshalling yards at Valenciennes, 25 miles (40 kilometres) north, and 30 B-25 Bostons of 2ndTAF attacking rolling stock and locomotives at Blanc-Misseron, 15 miles (24 kilometres) east. Fighters from 401, 402, 403, 411, 416 and 421 Squadrons provided escort and cover for the bombers whose accuracy was described as good. There was no aerial opposition, and while a reduced escort accompanied the bombers back to the coast, 421 and three other squadrons swept the area 50 miles (80 kilometres) south of the bombing targets. Frank and his fellow 421 pilots noted everything they could to report to the intelligence officer upon their return. In the 421 ORB the 2 May entry read:

"Three or four large barracks seen on edge of wood south of Rheuirs (sic) [Rethel?]. Several vehicles observed with personnel either loading or unloading equipment. Also numerous barges seen on river Marne just south of this area. Weather no cloud. Visibility good except in lee of small towns. Same over Channel."

Ramrod 831 on 5 May:

"This operation, which was scheduled for 0745 hours, was divided into several parts as follows: one attack each by Mitchells and Bostons escorted by Spitfire IXs on marshalling yards, two attacks by Typhoon bombers on Arras marshalling yards, two attacks by rocket projectile Typhoons on canal bridges and one attack each by rocket projectile Typhoons on Motteville Railway Junction and Tancarville Lock, and in addition a fighter sweep in the Lille area. ... The bombing results were considered fairly good."[†]

All the Spitfire squadrons of 127 Wing and 144 Wing participated in Ramrod 831, however only 443 Squadron of 144 Wing (fitted with the 90-gallon drop tanks to permit them to accomplish the sweep after the bombing) saw action — much to the dismay and envy of the 127 Wing pilots. In the sweep of the Lille area 443 Squadron destroyed four FW 190 enemy aircraft for the loss of one pilot.

In the first three days of May two pilots from 403 Squadron baled out over the Channel — both having been hit by flak — but fortunately, both survived unhurt picked up by search and rescue launches and returned to duty soon after. Then 7 May, on Ramrod 839 in which all three squadrons escorted Bostons to bomb a locomotive works at Valenciennes and then sweep far to the south, 403 Squadron got in a dogfight and two pilots made claims of two enemy aircraft destroyed and one damaged. The mission had taken the Spitfires to the limit of their range and the added fuel consumption in the dogfight resulted in a shortage of fuel that, in turn, resulted in one pilot baling out over the Channel, another just making it to the coast for a belly-landing at Beachy Head, another belly-landing at Friston and yet another having the engine cut out just as he came to a stop. Fortunately none of the pilots were hurt and all were back at the base

---

† DHH Day Fighter Narrative 73/829 May 1944, page 34.

that evening. Frank did not fly that mission, but the next day was to be his most interesting operation.

The 8 May mission that took off at 0605 hours, was officially dubbed a 'weather reconnaissance' flight, or as the pilots called them 'weather recces', but it was planned by the participants as a sweep looking for targets of opportunity. F/L Paul Johnson, an American from Connecticut who crossed the Canadian border to train in the BCATP, had just recently been promoted to command 'A' Flight. Johnson led the weather recce. F/O Bob Murray flew as Johnson's wing man; Frank flew in the number three slot and Hank Zary, another American serving with 421, flew his wing. The story of their exciting mission is recorded in several places. First the 421 Squadron ORBs:

> "Weather recce took off at 0605 hours composed of F/L Johnson, F/O Murray, F/L Clark and F/L Zary. They went into Cambrai area on the deck. Passing over a hill they met an Me 110 going in opposite direction. Johnson and Murray broke right, Zary and Clark left. Johnson and Murray fired at the bandit and Johnson destroyed him. Aircraft crashed in a field in the vicinity of Cambrai. On the way back, flight passed over aerodrome at Montdidier. F/L Clark reported seven Ju 88 aircraft dispersed about a mile from the 'drome. Our aircraft went down with F/L Zary getting a destroyed and Johnson getting a damaged. F/O Murray attacked a flak post and knocked hell out of it."

After final review by the intelligence officer, it was recorded that there had been one Me 110 destroyed in the air and three Ju 88s damaged on the ground (one credited to Frank). Paul Johnson's Combat Report stated[†]:

> "(a) Flying at approximately 50 feet in south-east-by-easterly direction near Cambrai, a Me 110 was sighted at 10 o'clock flying north-by-north-west. I broke to starboard to engage and closing rapidly opened fire at about 25 degree deflection. Strikes were observed along starboard wing inboard of engine. Enemy aircraft starboard wing tip struck ground and he broke violently to port causing my second strike to miss. On the third burst from dead astern number of strikes

† quoted in DHH Day Fighter Narrative 73/829 for May 1944 page 126.

observed and he crashed in a plowed field. F/L Zary saw the enemy aircraft crash and small fire (caused) the ammunition (to) explode. Claim Me 110 destroyed.

"(b) On Montdidier aerodrome five to seven enemy aircraft Ju 88s were observed dispersed in bays along south side of the field. The bays were sand-bagged on three sides. I dove down and opened fire on one of the enemy aircraft at about 800 yards, closing to about 200 yards. Strikes were observed and pieces flew off. Claim one Ju 88 damaged."

Frank also filled out a Combat Report staking his claim. Because he did not see the Ju 88 explode, he submitted the claim for one 'damaged' Ju 88. The combat report stated.

"There were five dispersal pens with a Ju 88 in each along the perimeter track on the south side of Montdidier aerodrome. I attacked the middle of the three diving from about 4000 feet, opened fire at about 1000 yards closing to 100 yards observed at least two strikes on fuselage. Fired 160 rounds cannon and about 500 machine gun. Claim one Ju 88 damaged.

signed F/L F J Clark

countersigned H K Martin senior intelligence officer 127 Airfield HQ."†

---

† National Archives UK document AIR 50/147 number 12.

Figure 18 — The official RCAF photographer's caption for this photo read; "Tousled hair after returning from an early morning patrol over France in which he damaged a Junkers 88, is F/L Frank J. Clark of Montreal in front of his Spitfire."

(CF Photo PL29567)

A week later Frank wrote the following letter. In one of his earlier letters Frank spoke of how callous people become regarding death during wartime, but in none of his letters to Bev does he touch upon the subject of how he feels about killing the enemy. It was not a topic that came to the surface readily because every pilot had some exposure to seeing the destruction of enemy aircraft or ground vehicles and must have thought about the humans in the machines and every pilot had lost a friend — many times seeing them die at close hand. In later years, when asked to comment, many pilots said there was a many-facetted experience that followed the sequence of intense feelings that played itself out each time they went on an operation. Nervousness and fright up to the moment of strapping in had to be fought each time they went out and there was no room for any other feelings. That nervousness grew easier to tame as time went by, but it was always there. With firing up the engine and taking off came the tremendous rush of adrenaline and the excitement of impending action. The excitement stayed at a high level throughout the mission but was jacked up another notch when they were fired upon or dove into action. When they shot down aircraft or destroyed trains, it was the equipment they destroyed, not the occupants. And that adrenaline rush lasted right through the terror and wild exertion of the dogfight or attack. It was only after, when an enemy pilot baled out or when the train crew fled under fire, that it was possible to think in terms of taking another person's life. All the pilots who talked of this in interviews long after the war, stated that there were two contrasting scenarios — either pure hateful murder perhaps after the loss of a buddy or the witnessing of some brutal act by the enemy, or a genuine revulsion at what one had done. Neither the hate nor the revulsion were things easily talked about and so the norm was to concentrate on the destruction of machines, not acknowledging that there were people involved. This called for a measured callousness that all pilots felt obliged to develop. In this letter Frank writes about strafing ground troops but behind the words one can sense the feeling of revulsion.

No one knew it at the time, but this would be the last letter Frank wrote.

"421 Squadron
RCAF England
May 16, 1944

Dear Old Joe,

I'm afraid I haven't written for a month now so thought I'd better dash off something — be it ever so scant and humble — to let you know that all's well on the European Front.

A month ago we left the old station that you never did get down to visit and hoisted our tents in another part of England, getting ourselves all ready to move off across the Channel come the invasion. Well, we're still waiting but I don't think we'll have to wait much longer. With the terrific air onslaught over France, Germany and the Netherlands these last few weeks, and with your big push in Italy well underway, I think the invasion in its preliminary stages has already begun.

In any case we haven't had much opportunity of being impatient in our outfit as we've been kept very busy these last few weeks. Since the first of May I've flown 14 ops sorties and have had more fun on them than on the 31 others I had done up to that time. We've been dive-bombing and strafing all sorts of military targets and generally raising hell whenever the occasion permits.

On one occasion, four of us went over deep into France at dawn one morning. We encountered an Me 110 and two of the boys shot it down while the other chap and I gave them cover. About five minutes after I saw five aircraft on an aerodrome which we attacked post haste. One chap claimed he destroyed one, another that he damaged one and I claimed a damaged (a Ju 88) although I'm hoping I may get it as destroyed after I've seen my cine-gun films. All in all, we had a damn good morning and exciting for a while over the aerodrome as they were shooting at us with everything they had.

The day after we got the 110 and the 88s we were down around Paris where four of us attacked and pretty badly shot up a truck and an immense trailer.

Two days ago we were out on an early morning show and after shooting up a couple of flak towers we sighted and attacked a big German motor convoy. We disabled about 10 trucks and half-tracks and killed scores of soldiers. We could see them running away from their vehicles as we dove on them and it was just like shooting snails. I saw one chap hit with a burst of 20 millimetre and just disappear. The squadron got a little mention in the daily papers for that effort.

Well that's about all the battle experiences I have to relate and I'm afraid that except for them I haven't much to fill up a letter with. I've been living a pretty quiet and consistent life since we started this outdoor life chiefly because I've been too tired at nights to do anything else but climb in between the blankets and sleep. Haven't been doing much thinking of things and stuff recently either which must be pretty well evidenced by this letter. Have been living pretty much of an animal existence all in all — working, eating and sleeping.

Hope you have received the books I sent by now. I still haven't finished the last volume of *War and Peace*, but don't think you can have finished the first two yet as I somehow imagine you have been working pretty furiously lately.

The two enclosed snaps are just to show you two things — one — myself with battle camouflage on (dirt and whiskers that are hard to keep removed with a limited supply of cold water) and generally scruffy clothes because I'm my own batman. The other is just to sort of remind you what a skiing weekend up north used to be like. Junie, Cynthia, Joan Postans and Marian (Beer) Gall went up one weekend in February and had a grand time. This is one of the snaps Junie sent me. You may be able to recognize the three of them as Cyn, Joan Postans and Junie.

At the moment I'm on a 48 in one of the towns near to our camp. Spent the first day of my 48 (yesterday) just lounging around the camp. Decided to come into town today and spend the night just to get away from things, have a bath, a couple of meals served with a bit of ostentation, pay through the nose for same, have a good sleep in a comfortable bed and generally have a bit of a change. Haven't hit the booze much (as yet) as I was on a terrific party which centred around 10 dozen eggs, two kegs and several cases of beer a couple of nights ago. We were released for the day so decided to have a bit of a do — so collected the material and started about 3 pm. By midnight Baachus himself would have been proud of me. I'm still sort of convalescing somewhat.

The hardest blow of all though was getting up for an early morning show the following morning. Although we weren't above 3000 feet during the whole show I used up half a bottle of oxygen — for medicinal purposes only. It is second to none as a restorative. It takes it out of you to some extent though by making you very tired afterwards. I was quite content to take my 48 yesterday which I really wasn't expecting. It's the first 48 I've had since the one I spent with Kenny in January. Haven't heard from him since then and haven't heard from old Joe Wilson for two months now. By golly, Joe, I miss you fellows. I think the only reason I haven't taken any leave for the past three months is that there aren't any Joes around to spend it with. Golly how lucky we were to have spent so much time together over here as we did. I guess you can't have everything — although sometimes I'd willingly accept same.

I'm getting impatient Joe for the day when we can all go home again — you to get married, Kenny to get settled in a good technical job, Tommy to rip around in great cars and little old self to sit around with a wife on one knee and the young son on the other. I'm getting a bit brassed off with life in uniform. It's almost four years for you and me now, Joe. That's an awful big slice to cut out of a young chap's life. Have you any idea what you want to do after the war, Joe?

I think about the easiest thing for us to do would be to stay in the services. They'll probably need lots of us as I anticipate a pretty large army and air force for a good while after the war. But the army is hardly a fit life or occupation for a young man with ideas. So I hope to gosh you don't decide to stay on. I'm pretty positive I shan't volunteer to stay on unless as a last resort to provide sustenance for Junie and Barry.

Imagine you have received your invitation to Jeanie and Ernie's wedding on June 10th by now. I wrote today wishing 'em luck and saying I was sorry I wouldn't be able to make it. I'm really glad to see those two get married at last. They're really made for each other I reckon and are two swell people.

Guess you and Mary will be next. That'll be another great day — am I going to be drunk — drunker still if I'm not there. That's the only way to get through the church ceremony, Joe, is to pack three or four away and get yourself feeling pretty merry — (and don't misinterpret that!).

Bit of news (which you probably know anyway) Gerry Racine was reported missing a few months ago but is back safe in England again and will be going back to Canada soon for a short leave.[†]

It's getting pretty dark and the light in this hotel room is pretty poor so I think I better make an end of this before I ruin my eyes.

Hope this finds you well and full of fight, Joe. You'll need it before your campaign is over. I hear Hal Carstairs was wounded. Watch yourself, Joe Baily. I want you back thumping the piano and floor at 4618.

All the best Bev, write when you get a chance.
Cheers.

Frankie."

---

† Gerry Racine was posted overseas about the same time as Frank and after OTU joined 263 Squadron flying Typhoons. He claimed three aircraft destroyed on the ground and four in the air, but was shot down in the last encounter 31 March. He evaded through Spain and Gibraltar and returned to the UK in early May 1944.

Frank had come into his own. He had learned to handle fear. He now had the experience to lead a section into battle and the confidence, derived from many operations, to get through complex situations like flying through flak fields, taking evasive action before bomb runs and facing enemy aircraft.

Back in January, Wally Conrad had marked Frank with an evaluation score of 44 points — almost none for operational ability because he had flown so little. By the middle of March, when Frank had 28 operational missions under his belt, the acting squadron commander, Ed Gimbel, gave Frank a score of 64. Now, in the middle of May with 45 operations under his belt, there was an evaluation performed by Graham Robertson, who had taken over command of 'A' Flight when Karl Linton reached the end of his tour. Robertson was about to be promoted to S/L of 411 Squadron four days later. Robbie's evaluation gave Frank a score of 78 — including highest marks possible for leadership in operations.

Just three days later Frank led Yellow Section on a mission called Ranger 127/32 — a sweep. 19 May was an eventful day for the wing as it flew three sweep missions. On the first of these, Frank flew Red 3 with Hank Zary his wing man. Six aircraft from 403 Squadron and six from 421 flew the mission. They crossed the coast at six in the morning and flew with a clear blue sky overhead and a bright sun reflecting off patches of heavy mist clinging in the valleys. It was a magical day. As they approached the Paris area they encountered a bit of accurately directed flak from Guyancourt airfield — one of the home bases of JG 26 — but no one was hit. At their first destination, Versailles, near Paris, they turned and swept the area 75 miles (120 kilometres) north-east to St. Quentin. Bathed in early morning sunlight, Paris looked like a fairyland. The first times Frank saw Paris from the air he mentioned them in letters to Bev, but on this mission it was even more beautiful. The two squadrons encountered no opposition, saw no other Allied aircraft and were back on the ground at Tangmere by 0720 hours.

Three hours later, with Frank leading Yellow Section, 421 Squadron carried out its second sweep by itself. This time the initial target was Dreux, 50 miles (80 kilometres) west of Paris. It was still clear with a slight haze to 3000 feet. The 421 aircraft crossed the coast at Dieppe and within three minutes, over Neufchâtell, four clusters of 88 mm flak burst all around them. F/L Dick Henry was flying Yellow 2, Frank's wing man, when his radiator blew off with pieces flying in all directions. As Henry's aircraft dropped out of formation, Frank and the other two members of Yellow Section, Benton Gilmour and Al Brandon, received Robbie Robertson's permission to follow him down. Henry glided with no power descending to 3000 feet where he baled out. His parachute opened at 1000 feet and he landed in an open field. As the three Spitfires orbitted, Henry waved and disappeared into a wood. Weeks later it was learned that he was captured almost immediately and served the rest of the war in a prison camp. Catching up with the rest of the squadron, Yellow Section flew south to Dreux and proceeded north-east to Beauvais without seeing any enemy aircraft and without any more flak. They landed at 1150 hours.

The last mission of the day — an unusual assemblage of seven aircraft from 403, seven from 416 and 11 from 421 — took off at 1800 hours bound for a sweep between Brussels and Rotterdam. Frank had his evening meal and was just coming downstairs to go to the Mess when he heard the droning of aircraft descending through the landing pattern and setting down. It was 1950 hours. Twenty minutes later the returning pilots were in the Mess drinking a toast to F/Ls Doug Lindsay and John Hodgson of 403 Squadron who each claimed the destruction of a FW 190. The mood in the Mess was restrained because one of the 403 pilots had to bale out over the Channel on the way back. He was listed as missing, his fate not yet known.

Throughout May there was at least one and many times three or four bombing Ramrods every day and all were escorted or augmented by the Spitfires of the ten Canadian Spitfire squadrons of 126, 127 and 144 Wings together with 402 Squadron. Dive-bombing became more prevalent in May as more and more 'No-ball' launch locations were identified by the aerial photo reconnaissance squadrons. The intelligence information correctly deduced that this terror weapon was about to become Hitler's scourge upon southern England when hundreds or even thousands of pilotless bombs might be launched daily. Operations Researchers concluded that heavy bombing was too inaccurate to efficiently destroy the small launch sites. Medium bombing was better, but best of all was dive-bombing. Within months it became apparent that the Hawker Typhoon — a large stable beast of an airplane — was the better platform to accomplish the bombing while the Spitfire ran a poor second.

By the end of May 1944, squadron-level dive-bombing missions accounted for one third of all their missions, with the remainder being evenly split, a third apiece, between sweeps and bomber escorts.

*   *   *

IT WAS THE Transportation Plan that led to one of the most ambitious, and most costly fighter sweep missions of this period. The date for this mammoth operation was set at 21 May when, in a mission called Ramrod 905, 1691 sorties[†] were launched in a massive 'train-busting' exercise. 24 squadrons of Spitfire IXs, eight squadrons of Spitfire Vs, two Tempest squadrons and two Typhoon squadrons were detailed to attack trains between the hours of 0700 and 1300 hours — and that was just the 2ndTAF effort. While 2ndTAF flew in Pas de Calais, Normandy and Brittany, US 9thAF flew in the Brest Peninsula and central and north-eastern France, and US 8thAF operated in Germany and Holland. 2ndTAF flew 388 sorties while US 9thAF flew 683 and US 8thAF flew 620 sorties.

First of all, the 2ndTAF attack was intended to knock out trains and train stations, but secondly, it was intended to confirm the Germans' unshakeable belief that the final assault upon Europe would be across the Pas de Calais — the shortest distance between the UK and Europe. So it was that as the sun came up, 144 Spitfires of the group with which Frank was familiar, swarmed like a cloud of locusts over north-western France; they were going to destroy every train they could see and every station and marshalling yard around. Trains that were knocked off the tracks or left completely enveloped in flames were classified 'destroyed' whilst all other conditions short of derailment were classified as 'damaged'. However, though the results were gratifying, the cost was very high. A total of 56 aircraft

† DHH Day Fighter Narrative 73/829 May 1944 page 85.

and 53 pilots were lost, but altogether the Allies claimed 159 trains and locomotives destroyed and 245 damaged. 2ndTAF lost 21 aircraft and 20 pilots; of these 127 Wing lost F/O Tommy Bryan of 403 Squadron who baled out and evaded capture, F/O Sten Lundberg of 416 Squadron who was taken prisoner, F/O Jimmy Davidson of 421 Squadron who was taken prisoner and F/L Ralph Nickerson who baled out and evaded capture.

Frank was thoroughly cheesed off that he had not been slated to go on this big train-busting mission, for he savoured this kind of a show. But he had flown on two missions two days before (one of which saw the loss of F/L Dick Henry, when he was hit by flak over Neufchâtell) and he flew the day before that, when they attacked a convoy of military vehicles and destroyed at least eight transports.

The number of missions increased in May, bringing continued pressure on the German defences from the V-1 launch sites in north-west France to the U-boat harbour at St. Nazaire. Frank flew a sweep of Fourmelot the evening of 22 May, escort to medium bombers hitting Lille airport 25 May and bombed a No-ball target 27 May.

*   *   *

I N THE FIRST year of its life (March 1942 to May 1943), 421 Squadron had destroyed only one enemy aircraft and damaged six others. But between June 1943 and the end of October 1943, the period in which Buck McNair enflamed them, the squadron tangled with the enemy every week. There were 23 encounters in which 22 enemy aircraft were claimed destroyed, one claimed as probably destroyed, and 8 damaged. The last battle in that period occurred five days before Frank arrived on 29 October when two Messerschmitt Me 109s were left smoking but not seen to crash. But while engagements had been so prevalent before, in the whole eight months of Frank's tenure with 421 Squadron, there were only three engagements with the enemy — the first was 3 November 1943, flying escort for 72 Marauders, at St. André de l'Eure the squadron shot down one Focke-Wulf 190, one Messerschmitt Me 109, probably destroyed another Me 109, and damaged another Me 109. Frank was still getting checked out on Spitfire Mark IXs when this dogfight occurred. The second engagement was 20 December 1943. On a fighter sweep over Merville the wing encountered 38 enemy aircraft. 421 Squadron shot down six with one probable and two damaged in the battle that saw the squadron leader shot down and killed. The third was 8 May 1944 when one aircraft was destroyed and three damaged near Montdidier. As noted earlier, Frank damaged one of these enemy planes. Late in May — the day after the train-busting exercise — 416 Squadron claimed the destruction of four enemy aircraft, but there were no more victories for 421 Squadron in the days before D-Day.

2ndTAF flew a few four-aircraft coastal patrols in the first days of June protecting the assembling Allied armada — and on one of these a 416 Squadron pilot was lost in the Channel after engine malfunction — but the general feeling was one of hiatus. Everything seemed to be holding its breath. Ed Gimbel left the squadron the first of June. 421 Squadron flew no operational missions in the first two days and only one in the first five days. That mission was Ramrod 962 just after noon on 3 June. Frank led Blue Section with Bob Grigg flying his wing man. It was a two-squadron sweep with 403 of the roads in the St. Lô and Carentan areas. The squadron ORB said of it:

> "Sweep of roads Vire/St Lo/Carentan/Coutances. Goods train travelling north from Arial T.5575 attacked from east to west. Stopped Cat B. No. three and five cars were flak. One staff car, one 30 hundred-weight solid body lorry travelling west from Gate T.4587, attacked, left in ditch. Five petrol cars seen in station at St Lo. One small truck attacked south of Marigny travelling east, left in ditch. One car attacked and left stopped south-east of Cainay travelling north. One staff car travelling west from St Lo T.330690. Two light trucks – yellow and khaki camouflage. One goods train standing in siding Goringy-sur-Vire T.575553 Cat Q. One goods train Aimel T.812746 Cat B. Large emplacement flak with buildings on Du Lance off Isles St Mercouf. Heavy flak Longueville T.7188."

Frank was undoubtedly having the time of his life on this mission for he often said how much he liked attacking trains and ground vehicles.

Chapter Eight

INTELLIGENCE briefings in the days before D-Day prepared the pilots for the expectation of high casualty rates. Some suggested as high as 40 percent in the first weeks of the invasion. A rate like that meant 12 of their 30 pilots might be lost — killed, wounded or taken prisoner. And considering that 421 Squadron lost three pilots and three aircraft between 19 May and 21 May, that figure seemed plausible. The three survived, but all were shot down by flak. Now it was expected that the action would be by both flak and enemy aircraft with the Germans mounting 1000 defensive sorties a day. There was great anticipation that D-Day would usher in the greatest air battle since the Battle of Britain.

D-Day chatter was the centre of all conversations around the pilots' dispersal in the days before 'the big show.' During the day of fifth of June, all aircraft were painted with 'invasion stripes' and a midnight briefing was held. The squadron assumed readiness at dawn of the sixth — D-Day. The plan was to have six squadrons of 2ndTAF Spitfires and three squadrons of US 9thAF Thunderbolts over the beaches from sun-up (0430 hours) to sunset (2250 hours). This entailed employing a total of 39 squadrons of Spitfires and 14 squadrons of P-47 Thunderbolts. Frank's wing provided three squadrons that flew four times each day as their part of this beach patrol effort.

The wing flew four patrols on D-Day and Frank was on the second at 1125 hours and the last at 2140 hours. All patrols were two hours duration over a path the length of the Western Assault Area of the beachhead — the 30 miles (50 kilometres) between Port-en-Bessin and the coast off the Cherbourg Peninsula near Valognes. Apart from Allied aircraft in frightening abundance, and the exciting action played out in the beachhead below, the patrols were completely uneventful. There wasn't a German airplane to be seen. The debriefing at day's end included an intelligence report that only two units, JG./26 and JG./2, had responded to the vast Allied aerial invasion, but that 20 or more units would be rushed to the Normandy sector within a few days.

Because they were so pumped up, it came as a shock when nothing happened on that first day. Only a handful of Luftwaffe aircraft were in the air over the beaches on D-Day and no one saw them. In the weeks following D-Day they rarely appeared over the beaches. They preferred to launch as many bombers as they could muster to attack the landing beaches at night, and to send forty or more fighters at a time to cover major moves by the army inland — well away from the beaches. In the face of the 30-to-1 superiority in numbers of the Allied air forces, this was a necessary strategy — who could blame them? In that first day the Luftwaffe only flew 319 sorties, although they soon upped that to 600 a day. They lost only 22 aircraft whilst the Allies, who flew a grand total of 14,700 sorties of which 5800 were fighters, fighter-bombers and medium bombers, lost 66 that first day.

The next day, D-Day-plus-one, the wing repeated its four patrols and Frank flew the 1125 and 2140 hours missions again. On the second patrol of the Western Assault Area Frank flew as Conrad's wingman in Red Section. That was the same as the day before but this day was tragically different. They flew inland from UTAH beach and dispatched a section to take out five trucks and a bus and then two cars and several trucks at Lessay. Near the end of their shift, at 1300 hours over UTAH beach, F/L Johnny Drope's aircraft MJ554, flying in Yellow Section led by Hank Zary, suddenly experienced engine failure. Since UTAH beach was crowded with the soldiers and equipment of the last of the 4th US Infantry Division and the advanced elements of the 30th US Infantry Division assaulting force, Drope was advised to bale out immediately and he proceeded to do so.

He was only a kilometre off the French coast and everyone expected, with literally hundreds of ships all about, that Drope would barely get his feet wet. Watched by all those close enough to see, Drope rolled over, cleared his aircraft cleanly, and fell out. But his parachute streamed like a long ribbon, never opening, and Johnny Drope of 421 Squadron, one of the most sociable and respected pilots in the wing, plunged 3,000 feet to a violent death in a shower of spray that rose higher than that of his Spitfire when, a half-of-a-mile away, it plunged into the sea. Death for many pilots was obscure, occurring out of sight of friends and confrères, but this was immediate. In full view of the pilots of 127 Wing, this futile, senseless death stunned every breast. Frank was horrified; he knew Drope well and liked him immensely.

Standard practice — especially on these first two days of beach patrols — was to have each squadron launch 13 pilots, squadron strength of 12 aircraft plus a 'spare'. If all went well and the other aircraft got off the ground and were functioning well, the thirteenth pilot would leave the squadron a few miles out in the Channel and return to Tangmere. For the first patrol that morning F/O Al Brandon was the spare for 421 Squadron. When he returned as the redundant member of the patrol, his aircraft was functioning in excellent manner — only needing a top-up of fuel before it could set off for the next patrol. Since the ground crew went to great lengths to ensure that the most flight-worthy aircraft at any one moment in time were always those set aside for the next operation, what a cruel irony it was to know that Drope was lost due to malfunction when Brandon's aircraft was fine. Ground crew became very distraught when they thought about such things.

Figure 19 — This photograph of 421 Squadron was taken at Tangmere 1 June 1944. Back row: F/O Grigg, F/L Grant, F/L Gilmour, F/L Clark, F/O Smith, F/L Paterson, F/L Johnson, S/L Conrad, F/L McElroy, F/L Zary, F/O Warfield, F/L Thorne, F/O Murray F/L Wilson. Front row: F/O Tetroe, F/O Curry, F/O McRoberts, F/L Stronach, F/O Bamford, F/O Driver, F/O Brandon, F/S Saunders, F/O Calvert, F/O Cook.

(Brandon collection)

On the fourth patrol of that same day, D-Day plus one, the designated spare for 421 Squadron was F/O Bob Grigg. He took off with the other boys, was assured all was well and then reluctantly told the gang he would see them when they came back from patrol. Flying alone back to Tangmere, something happened. All the pilots, and ground control at Tangmere heard Grigg's muffled radio message of a single 'Mayday' but nothing more — he gave neither position nor explanation, nor did he repeat the Mayday. Aircraft were dispatched from Tangmere to the best estimate of where he might have been, based upon the time he left the rest of the wing and when his Mayday was recorded. The guess was about 12 miles (19 kilometres) south of St. Catherine's Point. Several aircraft took part in the search and the visibility was good enough that an obvious indication should have been discovered, but neither his remains, nor the remains of his Spitfire NH183 were ever found.

And those two senseless deaths were not the only ones in the cursed trail of events played out before the eyes of all the 127 Wing personnel. The very next day — D-Day plus two, 8 June — again over UTAH beach, F/O Bob Maranda of 416 Squadron, flying MJ929 was hit by flak and his aircraft started to smoke. There was quite a bit of German flak over the beaches, but this was far enough out over the Channel that it had to be considered a very lucky hit by the German gunner. Maranda said he was going to have to abandon his aircraft and again, as with Drope, Chad told him a rescue vessel would pick him up as soon as he splashed down. A sigh of relief went out as those close enough saw Maranda's parachute open properly and he appeared to have a normal descent and a normal splashdown in the water. But something went wrong. Minutes later the rescue launch pulled him out of the water dead — strangled by the cords of the parachute he was unable to release.

Three pilots killed uselessly in three days. Frank flew on each of those patrols and saw the deaths of Drope and Maranda at first hand and experienced the horror of losing Grigg to the cursed Channel. Amidst the steady drone of the engine as he kept darting glances in all directions, he couldn't get the images out of his head. The thought of it sent a shudder running down his spine.

Every pilot in the formation felt that shudder. Indeed, those monitoring the radio communications back at Tangmere and those tracking the radar blips on the control ships stationed out in the Channel felt that same shudder. The Channel was a killer: more good men died when forced to ditch in the frigid dark waters of the English Channel than were shot down by enemy action over it. Too many good men were swallowed. Most military aircraft of the day could not be set down readily onto a water surface even when it was relatively calm. Air scoops and the weight of powerful engines usually tipped the airframe up and pulled it under the surface leaving little time for the aircrew to escape. In choppy seas the situation was even worse for it was far more likely to plow directly into the face of a wave. There wasn't a pilot in the formation that did not have a friend or confrère who had died or barely escaped death in an attempted ditching, and even if a pilot baled out at a proper altitude, the Channel had a terrible record of snuffing out life. Every mission flown from England had to cross the Channel twice — over and then back — and every pilot to a man, breathed a sigh of relief after each crossing.

The next day, 9 June, was characterized by a long interruption of flying when the weather socked in early in the morning and heavy rainfall and insufficient ceiling did not permit a resumption of patrols until late afternoon. It was hours before those weather reconnaissance aircraft sent out to review the situation could get close to the French coast. At that point in time, weather radar was not available to record precipitation concentrations and localities. Shipboard reports were the most reliable sources of information. From these reports it was understood that the ceiling throughout that period was virtually at sea level. Only after 2000 hours when the ceiling at Tangmere was 4,000 to 5,000 feet and when the meteorologists aboard ships reported an 800- foot ceiling over the beachhead, was the wing detailed to fly a patrol over the Western Assault Area.

As they approached the coast, coming in under the ceiling, every gun of the Royal Navy opened up and unleashed a furious barrage at them. The Spitfires quickly backed off, swore profusely over the radio and tried to re-affirm their identity by firing the proper IFF flares of the day and by exhibiting the distinctive elliptical shape of the Spitfire wing — from a great distance, of course. At the behest of Goodwood Ground Control, once again they approached and once again were driven back by anti-aircraft fire. This time the radio messages burned the ears of everyone from Operations Control in Tangmere, 2ndTAF HQ at Uxbridge and Operations Control on the three ships stationed off the Normandy coast, but obviously not heard by those cold and wet gunners who were anxiously fingering the triggers of their anti-aircraft guns.

A third time Chad was ordered to approach the Royal Navy ships. This time the barrage of Royal Navy fire was so intense that it damaged Chad's aircraft slightly, damaged Don Shapter's more, wounded Ed Kelly with shrapnel in his buttock and worst of all, sent F/L Bill Williams in MJ827 streaking down to the ground trailing smoke. Williams managed a crash-landing in German-held territory near Valogne, but he was severely wounded in the crash and made a prisoner of war. The German troops who captured him and the German medical staff who attended to him, took him to a hospital in Cherbourg. Bill Williams was still a patient in the Cherbourg hospital when the American forces liberated that port 29 June.

Frank flew two of the four patrols flown each day 6 June through 8 June. The weather turned bad Friday 9 June and only one patrol was flown — Frank was not on that one. But on the Saturday 10 June, of the four patrols flown, Frank was on three of them. He had found a new aircraft — NH415 — and he flew it on each of these patrols. All were uneventful in terms of enemy fighter action but the third patrol brought forth this entry in the ORB:

> "More patrolling of the Western Assault Area. Boys getting fed up with these uneventful patrols. Apparently there is no enemy aircraft in the sky at all. On the third patrol of the day, F/L P.G.Johnson's aircraft was hit in thirteen places by flak but he managed to get back to base where the damage was inspected and the aircraft promptly written off. Returning from flying spare on the third patrol, P/O J.H. Tetroe, a new pilot, undershot the runway, sheared off his wheels and burst into flames. Johnny managed to get out with only slight facial injuries but the aircraft was completely written off."

Because of no enemy opposition, on 11 June, the wing cut back to two-squadron rather than three-squadron patrols, but still flew four times. Frank flew three patrols, the 0635 hours patrol, the 0940 hour patrol and the last at 1735 hours. On the first of these, Frank landed in France with the squadron and 403 Squadron at B.4 Beny-sur-Mer after being fired upon by Royal Navy gunners. The aircraft were refuelled and took off on another patrol 40 minutes later. Weather conditions were appalling, there being complete cloud cover with the ceiling over the beaches and over the Channel of a mere 100 feet. They returned to Tangmere. Late that afternoon 421 Squadron flew one other beach patrol the conditions being little better.

Monday 12 June saw three two-squadron patrols and two single-squadron patrols flown, several of which touched down in France at B.2 Bazenville or B.3 Ste.Croix-sur-Mer on one of the patrols 421 Squadron and 403 Squadron took off together at 1530 hours, but while 403 then proceeded to provide cover for a convoy, 421 flew a beach patrol, landed at B.2, refuelled and returned to Tangmere. The 421 ORB said:

> "Another day of routine patrols arrived, with this squadron doing two. They landed in France again (refuelled and returned almost at once) and as the landing strip we were using is very dusty, the boys returned looking like grey ghosts and the aircraft were covered in dust."

Altogether, in those seven days between 6 June and 12 June, Frank flew thirteen times — 26 operations hours added to his flight log..

That night at a briefing, Chad summarized what the wing had been doing and what lay in store. Every pilot in the wing was doing a lot of flying, but the absence of aerial opposition over the beaches, evidence that several ALGs were ready to receive aircraft and confirmation that they would move to the continent within a week, led to some experimentation. For the next several days they flew two-squadron patrols and they touched down once at one of the new ALGs to re-arm and refuel before returning to Tangmere. This was accompanied by some patrols where they didn't touch down at an ALG. Landing at an ALG gave the pilots a chance to once again get used to the whine and irregularity of a metal tracking runway

— something they had not experienced since October of last year — and a chance to hear the exploits of the 'A' Echelon group under W/C Brown who had gone over the day after D-Day. Compared to the concrete or smooth grass runways of Tangmere, the tracking was a bit of a shock. At best it was slippery and gave off a horrible, high-pitched whine when aircraft took off or landed, but at worst it could break at the seams or places clamped down by attaching cleats and puncture tires with gay abandon.

Tomorrow, 13 June, was going to be different. Two squadrons would fly over to B.2 early in the morning, operate out of the ALG all day and return to Tangmere in time to set down before sunset. Chad gave the pilots the planned take-off times for the three patrols planned for the day — 0730 hours, 1200 hours and 1645 hours — with the ferry flight home to Tangmere planned for 1945 hours that evening. He mapped out the patrol routes and gave the day's call signs, flair colours, emergency bases and radio frequencies. He then invited a meteorological officer to describe expected weather conditions over the Channel and over Normandy — the weather would be heavy cloud all day with ceiling about 3,000 to 5,000 feet, perhaps a little rain but normal strength westerly winds. Visibility would be good. With each change of topic Chad had a humourous phrase to illustrate the point.

Conrad would command 421 Squadron with the code name 'Lovebird' leading Red Section. Clark would be his number 2 flying his wing whilst Gord Driver and Gord Mayson would fly Red 3 and Red 4. 'A' Flight commander Paul Johnson would lead Blue Section with Gord Smith, Scotty McRoberts and Lorne Curry flying Blue 2, 3 and 4. 'B' Flight commander John McElroy was having a deserved rest today, his place being taken by Hank Zary who would lead Yellow Section with Bob Murray, Roger Wilson and John Hamm flying Yellow 2, 3 and 4 respectively.

Neither S/L Freddie Green the squadron commander of 416 Squadron nor the 'B' Flight commander F/L Danny Noonan were flying that day — like McElroy, they both had a day off. Instead, the squadron was led by F/L Dave Prentice the 'A' Flight commander flying code name 'Tabbycat' Black 1 with Dave Blackstock, 'Black'

Campbell and Bill Saunders flying Black 2, 3 and 4. Don Hayworth, 'Mush' Sharun, 'Sandy' Borland and Dick Forbes-Roberts flew White Section, while Bill Mason, 'Cuthy' Cuthbertson, Bob Simpson and Pat Patterson flew Green Section. Chad Chadburn flew as a fifth member of black section in the capacity of both wing leader and 416 Squadron commander. His call signal was to be Tabbycat Leader. Because his regular Spitfire was in maintenance, Chad flew in Freddie Green's aircraft MJ824. The ground crew had not had time to paint his signature 'LV-C' on Green's aircraft and so it bore the identification 'DN-A'.†

Everyone to a man turned in early for they knew that the next day would be a long one — perhaps an exciting one — and there would be an early start, up at 0600 and take-off at 0730.

*　　*　　*

AFTER he finished the briefing, Chad left the auditorium, went outside and walked in the damp darkness. He had been back in action just two months — just waiting for the preparations to be completed, D-Day to be launched and the biggest battle of his career to get underway. It should have been like a dream fulfilled — it should have been like he was back where he really wanted to be. He should have been exhilarated to know he was once again doing what he did so very well. Instead, he was not himself, not exhilarated, more indifferent than anything. Things were not unfolding as they should: back with his comrades, back flying Spitfires — like the old days just months before. It should have been the happiest time of his life, but it wasn't.

It had been a long war for Chad. He joined up in May 1940, received his wings and his commission in October and was overseas the next month flying Hurricanes with 2 RCAF Squadron in December 1940. Two long and hard tours of duty had grown in intensity and in satisfaction as Chad rose through the ranks to command a flight, to receive a DFC, to command a squadron — the first graduate of the

---

† One of the perks of being W/C(F) was to have your initials replace the squadron code on the winco's personal aircraft.

BCATP to do so — and to receive a DSO and eventually to command a wing consisting of two squadrons. The end of that episode in his life came with the award of a second DSO. And upon completion of Chad's investiture by the King at Buckingham Palace, he was ordered back to Canada. It was March when he returned to Canada to receive great accolades and to be feasted and acclaimed by everyone. His job was to tour the country as a young conquering hero promoting the sale of Canada War Savings Bonds. What a disrupting thing that whole episode turned out to be.

Within days of being back in the UK, before he had time to digest the rude shock, he was ordered to take command of 127 Wing at RAF Station Kenley. The new orders were for him to lead three squadrons including the one he had grown up with, one in which he was still a part. He was to be W/C (F) for 127 RCAF Wing in command of 403 Squadron, 416 Squadron and 421 Squadron. This was more than he could have hoped for, so why wasn't he happy? Why did he feel things were working out so poorly? The answer was Nancy MacKay.

Chapter Nine

AT 0630 HOURS sharp, 24 pilots, two designated spares and various support staff descended the stairs, proceeded down the long hall and filed into the auditorium on the main floor.

The usual practice was to have the morning briefing sufficiently in advance of take-off to allow time for a good bacon-and-egg breakfast and for preflight ablutions. W/C(F) 'Chad' Chadburn greeted the pilots of 416 and 421 squadrons. Commander of 21 Sector, G/C William MacBrien or Base commander W/C Mannifrank Brown would normally have introduced Chad, but MacBrien was busy preparing to join the others in France later that day and Brown had left the base three weeks earlier to lead 'A' Echelon — the first of four echelons of 127 Wing personnel who would effect the move of the 850 personnel of 127 Wing from Tangmere to the new base in France.

Chad quickly repeated the times of the patrols, the call signs and colours of the day. The meteorological people had not changed the weather forecast — it would be nearly 100% cloud cover but visibility would be good. He repeated the names and flying position of all the pilots, wished everyone well and told them to get their bacon-and-egg breakfasts and be ready for take-off at 0730 hours.

*　　*　　*

FRANK HAD his breakfast and bicycled out to the dispersal hut, put on his parachute and Mae West and strode out to the waiting aircraft NH415. There he met Danny the ground crewman. Together they walked around the aircraft checking the red tape on the guns, starboard ailerons and flaps, the elevators, rudder and trim tabs. Frank stopped and urinated next to the tail wheel — both a necessary precaution and a good-luck move. He finished the inspection, chatting with Danny, checking movement of the port aileron and position of the flap, took his helmet with dangling oxygen and radio connections from the port cannon and put them on.

Danny helped Frank onto the wing root and saw him grab windscreen and canopy behind the headrest to vault into the tight cockpit. He settled his six-feet-one-inch height into the confined space of the cockpit until the parachute under him took the right form. Together they tightened the Sutton harness that secured him to the seat. Now came the standard routine. Frank closed the small side access door, clicked the fuel cock on, checked that the ignition switches were off, set the throttle open one inch, moved the propeller speed control lever fully forward, set the supercharger switch to 'automatic normal', closed the carburettor air intake, and set the priming pump to 'per temperature'. When he had completed these actions, he looked up and smiled at Danny who was standing on the wing root looking down at him intently. Danny straightened up, turned and hand-signaled the operator of the power vehicle to start up. Danny jumped off the wing root. Frank clicked the ignition switches to the on position and pressed the starter and booster coil buttons simultaneously — they called this 'pressing tit'. The engine gave a loud cry, ground for the briefest of moments, belched a large cloud of black smoke, coughed loudly and screamed forth its mighty roar. Frank throttled back and the Merlin engine settled into a beautiful steady rhythm. For a Spitfire pilot this was a song.

Because they had all done this so many times, and because they had often been drilled to perform this sequence of actions in quick succession, all twelve Merlin engines of 416 Squadron's Spitfires fired up in a mighty crash as did those of 421 Squadron. Each ear of the aircrew and ground crew listened intently for the steady rhythm of a healthy engine. The deep-throated thunder of the Merlins made every pilot's heart soar with a mixture of personal pride in their aircraft and pride in the powerful engine that drove it. Lately, there had been some difficulty experienced by some pilots in managing the smooth flow of fuel when switching from the 90-gallon auxiliary slipper tanks fitted under the fuselage to the aircraft's internal fuel supply. Two of the pilots of 421 Squadron had lost their lives only days before and the technical officers suspected both were caused by this difficulty. Confident that his aircraft was running smoothly, each pilot looked to the squadron commander for the hand-signal that would indicate it was time to roll out.

Chocks were pulled away from the wheels and the thirteen Spitfires of 416 Squadron moved slowly to get into a full line-abreast formation with half the aircraft on the concrete runway and the other half on the grass beside the runway. They throttled up to full power, rolled away, gathered speed, lifted tail wheels off the runway and took off. The 421 Squadron aircraft rolled out and lined up in the place vacated by the first line of aircraft. Conrad raised his hand above the open canopy and with a circular motion, signaled all 12 aircraft[†] to burst into maximum power. The aircraft accelerated quickly, pushed the pilots hard against the backrests, raised their tailplanes off the ground at eighty miles per hour and leapt into the air at 100 miles per hour. No sooner were they off the ground than landing gear were snapped up smartly. It was the signature of a good fighter pilot that wheels were raised the moment they lost contact with the ground.

The two squadrons formed into finger-four formation, climbed to 3,000 feet just under the uneven ceiling of cloud that blanketted southern England and set a course of 190. The 25 Spitfires passed over Selsey Bill and entered the fighter flight channel that led almost exactly a distance of 100 miles (160 kilometres) to Port-en-Bessin. Within the flight channel, they were immediately overwhelmed with the number of ships — even greater than on D-Day — and the number of patrolling aircraft. Everywhere, between cloud breaks, they could see numbers of P-38 Lightning aircraft of the US 9thAF, darting here and there in sections of four aircraft, flying protective cover for the ships. Air traffic was so dense and the ten/tenths cloud base so low, that they spread out — the standard procedure when flying into a mass of cloud — climbed through a solid cloud layer until they burst out into some open spaces in canyons between towering cliffs of cumulus. They climbed well above the cloud layer to 12,000 feet. Immediately out of the cloud they closed ranks to normal patrol distances and climbed to the planned altitude. The peaks of the clouds occasionally rose to 25,000 feet, but for the most part their planned

---

† At the last minute the 'Spare' had been cancelled.

altitude provided a clear view in most directions. The sky was a glorious color of deep blue with almost no haze between the cloud formations. They levelled out at 12,000 feet where another army of aircraft greeted them. They flew past many B-26 Marauder medium bombers from the US 9thAF formed into boxes of six aircraft each heading toward the continent. And no sooner were they past them than they encountered boxes of B-25 Mitchell medium bombers and several pairs of Mosquito night fighters of No.2 Group of 2ndTAF coming back after completing their assignments.

Frank took his hands off the doughnut-shaped control stick just to prove to himself that he had the aircraft as well trimmed as it could be and that it would fly itself — never wavering. The aircraft flew on in perfect trim. Then in a streak of perversity, he slid back the canopy an inch or two and amid the screaming airflow and increased engine noise, he held his gloved hand out in the open frigid air to the left for a brief moment. Immediately the Spitfire responded by swinging slowly around due to the increased drag. Frank laughed, slammed the canopy shut and corrected his heading. He rubbed his gloved fingers for it was at least 40 below outside his cockpit window.

Shortly after they had settled into a straight course at cruise speed, the radio set crackled, "Green 4 to Tabbycat Leader, sorry skipper, my engine's running rough and starting to overheat, afraid I'll have to go back."

"Tabbycat Leader to Green 4 — lucky we're not far from the sight of land under the cloud cover. Good luck, Green 4 and call if you need help. Over and out."

"Tabbycat Leader to Black 4. Please take over Green 4 position."

"Aye aye, skipper."

Pat Patterson of 416 Squadron dropped out of formation, throttled back and went into a long shallow dive. He hoped the dive might cool the engine and at least take some of the strain off it. Minutes later he was immersed in the thick cloud base. It seemed much longer descending through it than climbing into it had been only ten minutes before. Breaking out at the ceiling of 3,000 feet he found himself just a mile or two off the coast and pointed his Spitfire MJ770 towards

Tangmere. After a few minutes he reported that he was in the landing pattern at Tangmere. All was well.

The 127 Wing Spitfires flew on silently for several minutes and had barely gone 20 miles south of Selsey Bill, when the radio crackled a second time and an excited voice came over the air, "Mayday. Mayday. Lovebird Yellow 2 to Tabbycat Leader: my engine has completely cut out. I'm losing altitude and I can't seem to restart it: must drop out of formation."

It was F/O Bob Murray calling.

"Lovebird Leader to Tabbycat Leader, since we're a fair way out, request we detach two pilots to accompany Yellow 2 back to base." Wally's voice sounded very concerned. This sort of situation had happened too often before.

"Affirmative, Lovebird Leader, affirmative. Good idea. Over and out." Chad's voice too revealed an unexpected touch of concern.

"Lovebird Leader to Yellow 3 and Yellow 4. Find Yellow 2 and accompany him back to base. Good luck."

"Roger."

"Roger."

Conrad had ordered John Hamm and Roger Wilson to find Murray, accompany him back if possible, or stay with him so they could accurately report his position if Murray should have to bale out and end up in the drink. Again a shudder ran down Frank's spine as he recalled Drope, Grigg and Maranda.

"Tabbycat Leader to Goodwood Control: three of our aircraft are returning to base. Wilco, Goodwood."

"We are tracking them, Tabbycat Leader. Goodwood over and out."

"Tabbycat Leader to Lovebird Yellow Section. Lovebird Yellow 3 and Yellow 4, take care of Yellow 2. We'll see you guys tonight. Make sure the beer is cold when we get home after work. Yellow 1, please format on Lovebird Red Section. Good luck, chaps!" Everyone knew that English beer was never cold.

Murray had fallen out of formation and behind so quickly that it took F/L Roger Wilson and F/O John Hamm two or three minutes at full boost and diving — travelling at nearly 400 mph — before they caught sight of him. Murray's aircraft was perilously low and just barely visible through the dull haze ahead of them beneath the cloud cover. The propeller was not rotating and the engine had not restarted so he was gliding — losing altitude all the time.

"Yellow 2. Get out, get out!" shouted Wilson over the radio.

There was no response. The low cloud had no breaks, as was the case closer to the French shore and sinking wisps of cloud drifted down from the ceiling here and there causing Hamm and Wilson to lose sight of Murray's aircraft for a moment or two. Emerging from one of these wisps, they found the Spitfire had already gone into the drink leaving a great smooth smear of greenish foam and fuel spread over the waves at the site of the ditching. The Spitfire disappeared below the surface. They immediately reported their position to RAF Station Tangmere and requested an Air-Sea Rescue (ASR) Walrus be sent out. They began circling as close to the spot as they could. But all they could see in the choppy waves was a body floating face down — no dinghy, no wreckage and worst of all, no sign of life.

Hamm shouted, "He's there, right below me to my left, floating face down in the sea! No sign of his Spit. Must have sunk like a stone."

"I know. I know. I see him too. Looks like he was dragged down by his 'chute."

"Walrus ASR 53 on its way. We have a fix on your position. Estimated time of arrival six minutes," reported the recovery officer at Goodwood.

It was never determined for sure whether Murray got out of the aircraft — in which case he was likely much too low to have his parachute fully deploy — or whether, as Wilson suspected, Murray had mistakenly pulled the rip cord before he was fully out of the cockpit and was thrown clear with the impact of the ditching. That night in the Officer's Mess, when the whole wing sat stunned at the horrendous events of this day, the general opinion was that poor Bob Murray had been swallowed up by the bloodthirsty monster known as the English Channel before he could fully extricate himself from his Spitfire. But as events unfolded, the talk in the Mess that night centred around much graver concerns.

The remaining nine Spitfires of 421 Squadron and the 12 (including Chad's) in 416 Squadron heard all the radio transmissions. They listened in silent helplessness. Just as they approached the French coast, they heard the final radio transmission, "ASR 53 to Goodwood. ASR 53 to Goodwood: downed pilot's remains have been recovered and are aboard the ASR aircraft. I hesitate to report he didn't make it." Murray was dead.

Frank had become good friends with Bob Murray. He was a great big bruising westerner, but he was the most considerate guy you could meet. And he was tough. He could have bettered any man in the unit, but that wasn't his way. He didn't have anything to prove. You could just sense that he knew what was what and he did the thing that was best. Never had a bad word for anyone unless it was completely justified, never said ill of anything unless it sure as hell had to be condemned. Frank recalled how Murray was with Johnson, Zary and him on that Montdidier caper in early May.

Numbed by the suddenness and uselessness of this tragic event, the pilots completed the course to the French coast, descended to 3,000 feet while still out to sea to slip in under German radar and began their patrol. They turned west slightly inland of the coast, flew over OMAHA beach and Pointe du Hoc to Carentin, turned north-west, flew over UTAH beach to the coast near Valogne and then swung through 180-degrees to retrace their path. They flew in complete radio silence, not just because that was proscribed patrol procedure this close over enemy territory, but also because they needed time to digest the shock.

When Chad, the eleven pilots of 416 Squadron and the nine pilots of 421 Squadron finished flying their uneventful patrol of the Western Assault Area a little after 0930 hours, they formed up in a holding pattern off GOLD beach and landed two-at-a-time on the square mesh tracking (called SMT†) at B.2 Bazenville. Immediately, they

---

† The first ALGs constructed in the UK used Somerfeldt tracking, a wire mesh in long strips linked by longitudinal steel rods. This system was found to cause many tire ruptures and before D-Day was replaced by square mesh track (SMT) still found in great abundance today in the farm fences of Normandy.

were deafened by the high-pitch whine given off by the rotation of the undercarriage on the SMT steel wire mesh. They pulled off the main runway quickly onto dirt tracks and were guided by ground crew to halt in a defined dispersal area in order to allow the next pair to come in. Each pilot was then helped out of his aircraft and in ones and twos they trooped sullenly to the medium-size tent set out halfway down the mile-long runway into the Intelligence and Operations tent marked 'Int/Ops'. The servicing commandos immediately removed the fuel caps just forward of the windscreen and began filling the tanks with aviation fuel from Jerry cans while others began the ground checks of the aircraft, checking fluid and oxygen levels, mechanical and radio functionality, checking whether ammunition was full and checking for exterior damage from flak.

In pairs and groups scattered the entire length of the taxiways that paralleled the landing strip, there was another squadron of aircraft — Typhoon ground support fighters complete with their rocket rails. They were known as 'RP' attack aircraft because of their 'rocket propelled' weapons. This squadron was doing the same as 421 and 416 Squadrons, having arrived early this morning from the UK and destined to operate out of B.2 all day before returning to the UK tonight. They had already completed their ground attack against German armour near Chartres and were now re-armed and refueled waiting to embark upon another mission.

In the tent marked 'Int/Ops' the pilots assembled. Each had little to say; the only topic of conversation was to ask how this could happen to a wing as capable as theirs, to have lost another good pilot — five in all since D-Day, all of them dead (for though Williams was in fact in a German hospital, they thought him dead) without firing a single shot in anger, and without even seeing the enemy? How could this be? Were they cursed? Of course there was no answer. They were dismayed, if that is a sufficiently strong word to characterize their emotions, but had they been able to see what the end of this day would bring, they would have torn their garments in anguish, like Greek heroes and sprinkled the world with ashes, for this was to be a day of unspeakable consequences.

*   *   *

137

T HE SPOOK (air force slang for intelligence officer) confirmed the list of serial numbers of the aircraft of each squadron that were on patrol, the names of each pilot and the comments regarding the operation. The 416 Squadron ORB note was:

> "Patrolled Western Assault Area landed at ALG B.2 Weather, showers, visibility good."

The 421 Squadron ORB note was:

> "F/O R W Murray turned back with engine trouble and en route crashed into the sea. He was accompanied by two other pilots who after orbiting saw his body floating in the water, and returned to base. Other nine aircraft landed at B.2, weather 7/10ths to 10/10ths, cloud base 2,000 feet."

Both squadron commanders and the spook signed off the reports and the pilots left. Some of the them just stood outside the Int/Ops tent looking stunned and solemn. One of the four flight commanders admonished a recalcitrant pilot who had not flown perfect cruise order and was lax upon take-off. The words were empty and the ranting abuse lacked direction. It was a sham. The real fault was fate — or circumstance, or bad Karma, or just plain lousy luck. The other pilots who escaped the emotional outpourings of a frustrated leader, wandered about the new base in ones and twos noting what changes had taken place to B.2 Bazenville (as it was now officially called) in the day or two since they had first landed here.

The electrical system was now fully in place, with landing lights buried beside the SMT tracking all the way down the runway and many hooded lights mounted in convenient places in the maintenance and armament areas. Several more anti-aircraft gun installations dotted the perimeter surrounded with four-foot blast protection walls of stacked sandbags, instead of being out in the open as they had been only days before. The servicing area over near the stand of trees in the northern part of the base, previously had only two large tents; now the area extended in under trees, spread out substantially and sported the framework of a tubular-spined hangar where repairs could continue in foul weather or during nighttime when, blacked out by tarpaulins, repairs could continue without revealing any light for the Ju 88s to zero in on. There were two new cranes parked beside the makeshift hangar ready to start more complex repairs such as complete engine changes or the salvaging of whole airframes.

But the item that received the most comment was the hulk of a crashed US 8thAF B-24 Liberator, its fuselage stripped of wings, which was now resting among the trees to the north-west of the strip. It had been moved from the far end of the strip where it originally came to rest, off to the last remaining portion of hedgerow in the southern part of the base. It was no longer a hazard for those who might overshoot the runway.

To the east, where there had been a scattering of tents for the servicing commandos and the engineers — perhaps 50 or so — there were now row upon row of two and four-man tents, hundreds of them, and several huge tents for the kitchens, medical dispensary and non-com and officer's mess tents. And to the south-west, there were now clusters of tents for the radar and radio experts of 83GCC (83 Ground Control Centre) and right beside the runway, the tents, bivouacs and lean-tos of the medical staff who were evacuating the British and Canadian wounded. All of these additions made the airfield look very much more like the small village in the fields near Tangmere that housed the whole 127 Wing, but unlike the open fields of Tangmere, here they were distributed among the rows of apple trees in the orchard. The considerable growth and complexity of this developing air base in such short time was hard to believe.

Figure 20 — W/C Lloyd Vernon Chadburn, DSO and bar, DFC, C. de G., L. d'H, is shown in front of a Spitfire of 416 Squadron. Chadburn commanded that squadron on his second tour but at the time described here, he was W/C(F) of 127 Wing.

(CF Photo PL20344)

While they were taking a tour of the base, the 12 Typhoons of 184 Squadron came to life, taxied to the SMT metal tracking and took off — in twos, one pair behind the other until all 12 were airborne.

Chad came out of the Int/Ops tent and immediately searched out W/C Brown. He paid his respects to him and to S/L Scott, the wing Padre, and exchanged a few niceties with the other administrative officers. Then he excused himself to go to the latrine. It was here that a man had to face himself: there was no place for facade or the defensive layers of rank or privilege. Chad had always found he was the true person he believed himself to be here, in a john. With his pants down, every man was equal. His thoughts wandered from the terrible images he had seen.

He remembered the wild delight he and Nancy MacKay experienced at the end of last year when he was taken off operations and was lucky enough to be stationed at RCAF headquarters in London. From the end of December through February, each day he couldn't wait to break away and drive down to Hawkinge to be with her. He would have liked it to be every day, but in reality, the pressures of work permitted him to get away only once or twice a week usually in a stolen moment — perhaps more precious than a planned one.

It was at the peak of this period of intense passion when he was suddenly ordered posted back to Canada to go on the Savings Bond tour. The order came like a bolt of lightning out of the blue. He neither wanted it nor expected it. In his mind he thought he should have been treated better. The standard 'tour' was 200 hours. Chad had put in 350 hours on his first tour and nearly 200 on his second — surely he deserved a little 'special' consideration. Both Chad and Nancy were dumbstruck. Dumbstruck, no; Nan was devastated. She saw this as a termination of their relationship at a time when it had just begun to flower, and she made him promise he would come back for her. It had never entered Chad's mind that he wouldn't come back for Nancy but he was shocked at the nature of the posting. Chad never thought of himself as a performer and he couldn't picture himself on a stage with a troop of performers traipsing from town to town like a bunch of gypsies selling bonds.

The day came when they must part — Nancy was working on a second shift because flu had taken a terrible toll of the control centre WAAFs who were essential to the continuous functioning of the Operations Control Room at Hawkinge. She barely had time to talk to Chad and wish him well on his return trip. Chad left for Canada with only the shortest of communications with his beloved. In his mind he would do his duty back in Canada and get back here as soon as he could — no more than a few weeks.

Back in Canada the whole operation turned out to be quite different from what Chad had imagined. First there were the delays — nothing seemed to go as planned, but always a few days later. However, between 17 March and 4 April Chad spoke in 13 different cities and towns in eastern Canada, the furthest west being in Fort William. His ideas of what this tour might be were quickly dispelled. Instead of the bunch of gypsies he imagined, the presenters were intelligent, likeable people and the presentations and speeches were much more upbeat and serious than his 'gypsy' image. The presenters were very effective and very professional. The most difficult thing for Chad was the continuous pressure upon him placed by the presenters and the audiences to be a celebrity. By nature, Chad always played down his own accomplishments and those of his colleagues. It was a maxim of the times and a credo amongst air force officers that one did not brag but rather minimized or ignored discussion of one's achievements. But the crowds didn't want to hear this humility; they wanted him to tell them how all the boys handled fear and horror and death; they wanted Chad to go into detail — even exaggerate a little if need be — about the bravery and courage of 'our Canadian boys' in battle. At first he hated the attention, the constant praise and the pure adulation expressed by everyone he met. The whirlwind nature of the cross-Canada tour and the great outpouring of applause overwhelmed him and there was no time to do anything but perform. But of course the open hero worship that so characterized every appearance he made was a wonderful ego builder, and soon Chad felt he rather liked it. Before long he found he was playing to the crowd and enjoying it. The appearances became more satisfying until that singular moment when it struck him, like a burst from the blue, that he was doing something completely out of keeping with his convictions — something completely wrong. The young men who thronged to the defence of Great Britain in the terribly dark days of 1939 and 1940 were a generation who grew up without doubting their political and spiritual leaders. Their motivation was clear, precise and unshakable.

The Nazi party captured the hearts of Germans because it violently opposed the overly harsh burden of war reparation payments that had been imposed upon Germany by the Allies after the First World War. But while sympathetic to the cry for justice, all the world's peoples recognized the agenda of hatred and oppression they preached was pure evil. The invasion of Poland was accomplished by such lightning strike military might that most countries were intimidated. Things moved quickly. Britain and France declared war on Nazi Germany, but from the outset Britain had much concern regarding the resolve and effectiveness of the French military. There was no concern regarding resolve in Britain where Winston Churchill stirred the hearts of the British people and those of the Commonwealth countries by committing to fight the Nazis unto death. And when France fell in the spring of 1940, and Great Britain stood alone to face the tyranny, Churchill molded the resolve of the British people into defiant commitment. Young Canadians flocked to recruiting centres not only as an expression of support for the British Commonwealth, but because they knew the totalitarian threat could spread around the world, and while many nations condemned the Nazi action, only Great Britain stood up to stop them. These young Canadian men who joined up saw it a moral duty to take a few years out of their young lives to eliminate the evil that was Adolph Hitler and his party. So the thought that came to Chad — so much like a bolt of lightning — made it clear to him that here he was in Canada, soaking up fame and adulation while what he should be doing was getting back to winning the war with his fellows. He determined to return to the fight immediately.

Although he tried to steal time to write to Nan while on his tour, he wasn't very successful and wrote only a couple of letters — not nearly as many as he planned. Nan couldn't write either. Her job was in the operations room at Hawkinge ground control and that vital function often called for the WAAFs to work round-the-clock — especially if one or two other WAAFs were sick. The early winter months were very severe in the UK and there always seemed to be several WAAFs off sick. Nan avoided the flu and serious colds, but that meant she worked longer hours filling in for missing workers.

As soon as the tour ended, Chad begged the RCAF brass to send him back overseas, not so much to be back in the fighting, for he was getting a bit weary of it, but to see Nan. The government had one more function for Chad to perform — have his portrait painted in Montreal. That gave him a chance to see his brother Ford and to visit the Russel family, parents of Hugh and Dal, his two best friends. But it would entail another delay in getting back to Nan.

He finally got his way and flew back to the UK in early April as a passenger on the ferry flight of a B-24 Liberator. Landing in Lincolnshire, Chad wangled a flight to London, hurriedly reported in to HQ and immediately called Hawkinge to tell Nan he was back. What a shock it was to call the operations centre asking for Nancy only to be told that she was leaving to marry a naval officer. Chad couldn't believe it.

"How could she do that? She was going to marry me!" Chad exclaimed.

"This Nancy that is getting married, what is her birthday?"

"Why it's today. That's why we're having a party for her."

How could Nancy do this to him? Chad was heartbroken and became so depressed he didn't know what to do. He called his best friend Dal Russel, picked up a case of beer and the two drove deep into the South Downs where they spent the day getting very drunk. Two depressing days passed before the matter was cleared up when Nancy called. It had all been a horrible bit of miscommunication. Another WAAF named Nancy who, coincidentally had the same birth date, was the one who was going to marry the naval officer. Chad's depression vanished and he eagerly arranged to see Nan as soon as possible. But the shine had dimmed in their relationship. The shock upon the return was enough to shake Chad's feelings to the core and the long period of meagre communication dampened the intensity of the feelings of both of them. They began to argue and get angry at each other for the first time. Then officialdom entered the scene.

Chad was given command of 127 Wing and in mid-April moved the three squadrons of 127 Wing from RAF Station Kenley to RAF Station Tangmere. That made him twice as far from Hawkinge as he had been in his London position. They could not get together as often. The periods between their meetings grew longer and longer. And then when they had almost drifted apart, Nancy announced that she was pregnant. It was a shock. In those days having a 'baby-out-of-wedlock' was a major calamity for the families concerned; a disgrace of the first order. Neither Chad nor Nancy wanted a baby at this time, but it was unthinkable that they would not marry. They made every effort to try to recapture the feelings they had had before, but they both knew they were faking it.

While Chad was in the latrine, the other pilots lit up cigarettes, wandered around and tried to put the tragic recent events out of their minds. Some chatted with the servicing commandos. Several went into the large tent where S/L Crawford Scott, the wing padre, soothed their troubled thoughts and found consoling words that helped. He brewed some tea, apologized that there was no beer so far in the bridgehead and drank tea with the pilots. In the midst of this sober moment a siren wailed and over several Tannoy loudspeakers strung up in apple trees came the alarm, "Scramble! Scramble!"

From all corners of the base, pilots bolted out to their aircraft on the double. They climbed in, hurriedly checked out the instruments and started up automatically as ground crew provided start-up power. They lined up to take off two at a time. It took 15 minutes before the last aircraft was airborne — the later ones fearing they may be strafed before getting into the air. Between 1110 hours when the first two Spitfires lifted off, until 1125 when the last were airborne there was great anxiety for they were very vulnerable to air attack. The assemblage of Spitfires slowly formed up out over the sea and as soon as 416 was intact, Chad set off to the sighting location while Conrad circled waiting for the 421 aircraft to form up. Chad found nothing more than some spotting Spitfires directing naval gunfire and several far-off groups of American P-47 Thunderbolts dive-bombing. They climbed through the first layer of thick cloud, came out under another higher layer and passed through it as well. They found nothing.

Chad announced, "Tabbycat Leader to Shindig. We found no bogeys. Repeat zero contacts. Tabbycat and Lovebird will return to base. Tabbycat over and out."

The two squadrons returned to the coast off GOLD beach. Once more they landed two at a time and taxied to their dispersal parking spots.† Once more they congregated at the Int/Ops tent. They were told to stay close to the dispersal area because it was now 1140 hours and the next patrol was to start taking off at 1200 hours. 421 Squadron (Lovebird) would lead off first with 416 Squadron (Tabbycat) right behind.

---

† There is some evidence from the log of a New Zealand flight control officer that because of the fear of losing aircraft in a ground attack, 421 was directed to land at B.3 Ste. Croix-sur-Mer ALG, and although this makes very good sense, there is no corroborating evidence in the 416 ORB, the 421 ORB, 127 ORB or the 2ndTAF ORB.

Chapter Ten

RELATIVE quiet in the countryside between the sleepy villages of Bazenville and Crépon was shattered as Merlin engines boomed and became a chorus of deep-throated roars that filled the air. It was the start of the second patrol. Each engine gave out a grinding roll, a loud cough accompanied by a crash, a blast of black smoke spurting from the exhaust pipes, and then the settled down into the strong rhythmic growl of a well-tuned engine as the pilot trimmed back the throttles. Any one Merlin engine commanded respect when it roared in this manner, but 21 Merlins powered up at the same moment made one think it was the sound of the coming of the end of the earth or like an earthquake; perhaps the eruption of a volcano.

Figure 21 — A 421 Squadron Spitfire taxiing in preparation for take-off at B.2 ALG in France.

(IWM 792)

The two squadrons had started out with 25 Spitfires — 12 of them from 421 aircraft, 12 from 416 plus Chad's. Patterson's aircraft dropped out with mechanical difficulties at first and then three aircraft left when Hamm and Wilson headed back to Tangmere to try to accompany Murray. Now the patrol was down to only 21 Spitfires. Two-by-two they took off and headed to the coast to form up. By 1220 hours they were at 2,000 feet over the Channel just off the coast near Arromanches, circling to take up their places in a wing formation. When they were ready, they set out on their patrol.

All eyes strained to check every nook of the folded clouds around them and everything that appeared to move in the hazy ground below. Quick glances in one direction and a quick shift to another direction — that was what a fighter pilot learned to do instinctively. Without this vigilance there would be all sorts of unpleasantness. The whole sky and ground had to be continuously scanned; sometimes the curious colourings of the sky and the perennial ground haze obscured the most obvious sightings. Failure to spot the enemy first could mean he was on you in a flash.

This visual checking required such intensity that it usually meant that no pilot could think of anything else, but had to keep every ounce of attention glued to the searching. However, Frank found himself thinking some disturbing thoughts that crept into this intense staring.

Frank thought of the night-time conversation he had with Johnny McElroy not that long ago over how they wanted to die. It wasn't something most pilots ever talked about. Dying was for others. But both Johnny and Frank had had quite a lot of beer that evening and back in the two-man tent they had found themselves talking in the dark — remembering those moments that became obsessed thoughts. There were those moments when, entering a flak field over France or diving on a train with a thousand streams of flak racing up to hit you, that one wondered, for just a fleeting moment, is this it? Am I going to buy it right here and now?

The worst case for both of them was the dive-bombing. It entailed six aircraft kept clean to fly high cover to protect the other six that carried 500-pound bombs under the fuselage — one each. The six bomb-laden aircraft would approach the target at 6,000 feet in a line astern formation. The lead aircraft would fly until the target was under its starboard wing, peel off to the right, dive at 60-degrees while trying to hold back the buildup of speed to no more than 380 mph, pull out at 3,000 feet and release the bomb just after the pull-out. The second aircraft would then repeat this manoeuvre. By the time two aircraft had dropped bombs, the third pilot was certain that the anti-aircraft gunners on the ground had a very precise sight lined up to nail the next attacker. But there still remained a fourth, and often a fifth and a sixth. Being fifth or sixth was like walking into the valley of death — just asking to be blown out of the sky. All flak fields were terrible to endure but the dive-bombing operation was the worst.

"Almost everyone has been hit by flak at one time or another."

"I guess that's true."

"Sometimes it isn't so bad. You may not even know it until you get back and count the holes in the fuselage."

"Nevertheless, it sure is scary in those first few moments after your aircraft gets rocked by a hit, wondering if anything aboard is going to blow up or catch fire. And it's even scarier when you get back, thinking you haven't really been hit at all, to find a great hole in the fuselage and your oxygen bottle blown completely away. A shell in the cockpit area has got to be the worst thing."

"I once saw a fellow pilot with his foot caught in the canopy when he was trying to bale out. Terrible sight. He went in with his aircraft — never did get clear."

"I guess that's as bad as poor old Johnny Drope, having the parachute stream and never open."

"I was there. I never in my life saw such a terrible sight. I'll have nightmares about that moment for years to come. It was horrible — the worst thing one could imagine to happen to a friend."

"Wally Conrad had his parachute stream once. But he was pretty low to start with and came down into a huge pile of hay. He said he walked away with nothing more than a lost shoe! That was in France. The French Underground hid him and got him over the border to Spain and back to England by way of Gibraltar."

"I heard he was downed in France and got back without being captured, but I hadn't heard of the parachute streaming. It was an aerial collision, wasn't it? Hard to believe that he got away so lucky, but I guess that's the breaks. What happened to the other pilot?"

"It was Wally's wing man. He didn't make it. Like the other fellow you mentioned, he never got out of his aircraft; went down in the Channel. It was a tough break; he thought he could get back with half his wing gone."

"Yeah. Breaks have a hell of a lot to do with it."

"Some guys are lucky, some guys aren't."

They were talking in near whispers, but their voices floated between the two cots like smoke. The words seemed to have a special reality in the dark. Each felt that something important was being imparted: every word had to be weighed. Between each comment there was a long pause to let the words lodge in the mind and add images — each had a plethora of images. Frank remembered seeing a confrère pulled out of his cockpit looking like a barbecued chicken. There had been a fire in the cockpit — the Spitfire 90-gallon fuel tank located just beyond the firewall in front of the pilot had exploded. Every Spitfire pilot knew that the biggest danger in combat was fire that ignited the highly flammable fuel right in front of his face. Burns were a Spitfire pilot's biggest nightmare.

"I was down in East Grinstead once," said Johnny.

"The famous burn centre?"

"Yeah, Queen Victoria Hospital."

Frank had been there once too. His mind brought back images of the unbelievable acceptance of the townsfolk of East Grinstead as terribly disfigured men — always in complete uniform — were escorted around town by lovely young nurses and citizens who had learned never to flinch or show any outward sign when confronted by the horrible facial injuries that had been inflicted upon pilots and other burn victims.

"I think the worst way to go would be burning," said Frank.

A gesturing Conrad about 300 feet away suddenly brought Frank back to the minute. Wally was pointing up to the right. Frank followed the direction of the pointing but could see nothing. All pilots had to have very good eyesight but Frank was known to have truly exceptional vision. Frank moved his hands in a wiping motion indicating he could see nothing untoward and Wally responded with thumbs up. That put an end to Frank's lack of attention. This was not the time to daydream. If he wanted to stay alive he had better be alert and not let his mind wander.

They flew on, turning their heads continuously, straining their eyes to clarify anything that might turn out to be the enemy. After an hour of flying, a voice over the radio exclaimed, "Tabbycat Leader, this is Tabbycat Green 4. My engine is stuttering and the temperature has shot up. I'll try to set her down."

"Tabbycat Leader to Green 4. We're about 30 miles from base, but there are at least two other ALGs near here. Set her down before she seizes up ... and good luck, Green 4."

"Wilco, skipper."

Another engine failure! That brought the total to a half-dozen in one week. All the others appeared to have been fuel transfer problems — occurring when switching from auxiliary tanks to the main tank, but this one sounded different. Frank listened intently to his own engine, but the smooth beat reassured him that his Merlin was healthy and happy.

"I think that's Flight Sergeant Saunders flying in the Green 4 slot. I hope he can dead-stick into one of the landing strips, because some of these farmer's fields look pretty ploughed up, tricky to land in."

The formation of Spitfires flew over the Eastern Assault Area, travelling west to Port-en-Bessin and turning around and flying east over the British sector at GOLD beach, past the Canadians at JUNO beach and inland over Bayeux and Caen before turning north-east and flying up to Cabourg on the coast at SWORD beach. At this point they turned and retraced their path to Port-en-Bessin. One complete circuit took about eighteen minutes. They encountered heavy flak near Caen — heavy enough that at the low altitudes everyone spread out and took furious weaving action trying to avoid the bursts. There was also a surprising amount of flak just east of Pegasus Bridge where the Germans pinned down the British Sixth Airborne Division from advancing further. After four circuits they began to land in pairs at B.2.

Bill Saunders didn't make it to one of the landing strips but did find a good field into which he crash-landed; sliding along for 200 yards after coming in with wheels up at 100 miles per hour. He opened the canopy and shut down ignition and fuel before landing and immediately unbuckled and jumped out of the Spitfire the moment it came to rest. Luckily there was no fire and no explosion and it was only as he left the field and started to walk on a road leading in the direction of B.2 that he realized he had given his head a pretty good wallop and his left hand throbbed.

*   *   *

WHEN the two squadrons were safely on the ground at B.2 around 1410 hours, ground control told the pilots they had a fix on where Saunders went down and that a search party was presently driving to the area to pick him up. That was a consoling thought. They were all part of a team; everyone was concerned about everyone else. They had had one tragic loss, they didn't need another.

The de-briefing was short since there was nothing to report other than the weather — still 8/10ths to 10/10ths cloud cover all over Normandy, with a few rain squalls encountered shortly after take-off. They also answered the Spook's questions about where the ground action was so he could redefine where the Allied bomb line appeared to be.

"How much time have we got?" Gordie Driver asked.

"Next patrol take-off time is 1645 hours, so we have a couple of hours," Wally Conrad replied.

"Anybody care to do a little exploring for trophies around here?"

A burly Service Commando who was standing nearby said, "I wouldn't do that if I were you, sir. We cleaned out a sniper just yesterday and over there beyond the trees, see that flat section? That's a minefield still only partly cleared. Be best to stick to the airfield, I should think, sir."

"Er, thanks," replied Driver.

Conrad, Frank, Driver and George Mayson wandered over to the large tent marked with the wooden board 'Officer's Mess'. It was time to shoot the shit with Chad and the other pilots. As they trod along the dusty taxiway, a single Spitfire MkV landed.

"Looks like we've got Iron Bill MacBrien back to keep us company," said Wally.

They watched as MacBrien's aircraft taxied over the to the Ops area where W/C Brown and the few senior officers were waiting to

151

greet him. As they stood taking in the activity in every corner of the base, four Dakotas landed one after another at the airstrip and were directed to the group of lean-tos huddled a way down at the southern end of the airstrip. Frank and Wally squinted to try to make out what they were doing.

"Those are Red Cross trucks or ambulances down there aren't they?"

"Sure look like it. There must be twenty of them."

"Busy place this B.2," said Wally. "C'mon, I think I see Alex Hamilton over there, let's ask him what's happening."

Driver and Mayson wandered off somewhere — probably back to the mess. Frank and Wally walked over past the Int/Ops tent to a canvas-covered Bedford truck that had three stairs crudely fashioned to permit climbing entry into the bed of the truck. Over the entrance was a piece of wood with the words 'Chief Engineering Officer' painted in crisp black.

S/L Alex Hamilton described to them some of the hazards such as the ack ack from the guns at the field and also from the Mulberry harbour. As if to illustrate the point there was the clear sound of anti-aircraft fire coming from afar. Alex jumped up, went to the entrance, held back the fold of the canvas and looked all around.

"That's coming from the Mulberry at Arromanches shore line. It's only about three miles away, you know. Look through the trees over there and you can make out some of the balloons flying over each ship. The ack ack keeps us awake every night. Right after the sun has gone down, the Ju 88s come over every night to bomb the harbour. Our own chaps here at the field sometimes get a lick at them, but it's the Royal Navy gunners that just slam away constantly at the Jerry bombers. No shortage of ammunition I can assure you. Wait 'til you spend your first night here — it's quite an initiation, quite an experience, especially when the shrapnel from the ack ack guns drops white hot pieces through the sides of your tent."

"We were wondering what the Dakotas are here for. Are those Red Cross trucks we see at the other end of the strip?"

"Yeah. We tend to think that we only have our wing personnel and a few Servicing Commandos around here, but there are really many more. Right up until a day ago we still had a few soldiers from the Green Howards Regiment helping mop up the snipers. We had about three snipers that scared hell out of us. They finally got them

Figure 22 — Dakotas at the medical evacuation centre at the end of B.2 ALG runway. They flew in needed medication and returned to the UK carrying over 300 wounded soldiers a day.

(CF Photo PL30080)

"What you see is the airlift of the wounded. We get about 30 or 40 Dakotas coming in every day bringing in special medical supplies or any urgently needed item and flying out those wounded troops who must be flown back to the UK for special treatment. About 300 a day pass through here. The structures you see house some of the medical staff from 52 Canadian Field Hospital. The wounded are staged in the huts until the next Dakota flies them out.

"Hey, and that's not all. You saw the Typhoons of 184 Squadron who are operating out of B.2 all day, just as you guys are, but you missed 11 Spitfires of 66 Squadron who dropped in unexpectedly to be refuelled and re-armed while you guys were on patrol. Every day it gets busier.

"As to permanent residents, we not only have the medics there we have two lots of Servicing Commandos 3207 and 3209 — the specialist chaps among them are kind of interchangeable and rotate around between here and B.3 or B.4 — and we have 83 GCC and 410 Repair and Service Unit (410 R&SU). The Servicing Commandos number about 300 whilst 83 GCC group consists of about 50 personnel plus all their equipment located down in the village of Bazenville. When you're at the far end of the runway just past the medical airlift group, you can just make out the radar dishes and radio antennae through the foliage. They've just gone live today. As of now they'll take over complete control of all RAF and Commonwealth flights in the beachhead.† The 410 R&SU will arrive in a couple of days. They will eventually number a couple of hundred personnel and they'll look after all the Cat B repairs and they'll perform salvage operations of all downed aircraft."

"How was the crossing, Alex?" asked Frank.

"Maybe you didn't hear, but we had one of the two LCTs (Landing Craft Tank) torpedoed on the way over. We lost four men who went down with the ship — all from 3207 Servicing Commandos — and we had a couple of our boys wounded: burns and cuts, that sort of thing. The ship went down and the rescuers took all the survivors back to the UK. So we are pretty short of staff. S/L Cam MacDonald's medical team is missing three and S/L Fisher, the flying control officer and four of his men were all torpedoed. We don't know where they are right now, although we've been told they're okay."

Over the loudspeakers strung up on poles and in trees around the base a voice announced, "Pilots report to dispersal. Repeat. Pilots report to dispersal."

"I guess that's us, Alex. Again, many thanks."

---

† From D-Day until 13 June 1944, all ground control of Allied aircraft was performed by three specially converted ships called Fighter Direction Tenders (FTD) — HMS FDT 13 in mid-Channel, HMS FDT 216 covering the American beaches and HMS FDT 217 covering the British and Canadian beaches. On 13 June, FDT 13 and FDT 216 returned to the UK for repairs whilst FDT 217 stayed on another week until the American GCC was set up and operating at the American ALG A.2 Criqueville.

When Frank and Wally joined the small group of pilots standing around the Int/Ops tent, Chad was speaking.

"Visibility has noticeably deteriorated since our second patrol," announced Chad, "Time for our last patrol. Again it's going to be over the Eastern Assault Area; the Yanks seem to have the Western Assault area in control."

"Okay, guys, no suspected Huns lurking around, but let's go!"

And so it was that they took off on the most fateful patrol for the 2ndTAF forces in Normandy. It was a nothing-to-be-gained formality patrol that had no real impact upon the conduct of the war — a standard order that just required someone do it. Furthermore, it was to take place in such marginal weather that it might easily have been cancelled — but it wasn't.

*   *   *

ALL PILOTS from 416 and 421 Squadrons assembled near the Int/Ops tent waited for a truck to take them out to their aircraft. This was the last patrol of the day. 416 Squadron would leave their 90-gallon slip-tanks here at B.2 (the ALGs were short of them), fly in a clean configuration for one hour and land back at B.2 at 1745 hours. They would have an hour's rest while their aircraft were being serviced and re-fuelled and then they would ferry the aircraft back across the Channel to Tangmere leaving at 1900 hours.

421 Squadron would retain their 90-gallon slip-tanks on this patrol, stay aloft for an hour-and-three-quarters to perform an additional couple of circuits of the Eastern Assault Area, land at 1830 hours, shed their fuel tanks, have forty-five minutes off and then ferry the aircraft across to Tangmere leaving at 1945 hours. Staggering the length of the patrols was more in keeping with the longer time it took all 20 aircraft to take off or land here in the advanced landing ground where they could only handle two at a time.

Strapping himself into the seat of his Spitfire, Frank found this moment always exhilarating. At Conrad's signal the Merlins were fired up and at 1645 hours Chad led 416 Squadron up and out over the Channel, carefully keeping them away from the trigger-happy Royal Navy gunners concentrated at Arromanches. 421 Squadron followed. In fifteen minutes they had formed up with the 416 aircraft and started the patrol route — six miles (just over a minute flight time) west to make a landfall at Port-en-Bessin, inland about five miles, turn to the east 22 miles (35 kilometres) until the aircraft were south and east of Caen, then turn north-east, fly another 15 miles (24 kilometres) to Cabourg and then turn around and retrace their steps. The whole circuit was about 96 miles (154 kilometers) and took them about eighteen minutes. When they were just east of Bayeux — not yet halfway between Caen and Bayeux — ground control radioed.

"Shindig to Tabbycat. Shindig to Tabbycat: bogeys at vector 019 about 20 miles, angels 12. Current position U.2194. Bogeys heading vector 200 towards Mulberry. Repeat, bogeys in your sector heading towards Mulberry. Bogeys in your sector."

"Tabbycat reads Shindig: am responding. Over and out. Tabbycat follow me; Lovebird carry on with the patrol. Catch you later. Tally Ho."

"Lovebird to Tabbycat Leader: received and understood."

All the pilots looked to Chad's aircraft as it immediately banked and broke off to the north. The other 10 aircraft of 416 Squadron followed Chad's lead and broke as if one complete formation, leaving 421 to carry on with the circuit. Conrad and the other eight pilots approached Caen flying between 1500 and 2000 feet above the ground just under the cloud base. They flew well to the south of Caen to avoid the concentrated flak for which Caen was noted. Wisps of cloud hung down from the cloud ceiling like wayward children venturing beyond their mother's grasp. The Spitfires sliced through these wisps under the gloom of the overcast. They encountered no flak. Clear of the Caen area, the nine Spitfires turned diagonally left flying north-east toward Cabourg. Everything looked calm from the air and the grey-green fields refreshed by the gentle summer rain looked so peaceful it was hard to believe that tanks and troops and trucks were waging war down there. Chad had been gone about five minutes when they started to turn at the end of the circuit. Over the radio they heard Chad.

"Tabbycat to Shindig. Tabbycat is at intercept point. No bogeys. Repeat no bogeys. It was a squadron of P-47s. Tabbycat returning to patrol. Over and out."

The nine aircraft started re-tracing their flight path from Cabourg to the point south of Caen where they would turn west to proceed to the westernmost part of the Eastern Assault Area. Cabourg was experiencing a little rain shower and the ceiling was only 1200 feet. It was 1730 hours. Visibility was poor in the haze and scattered showers. Suddenly, a formation of aircraft was seen approaching them at the same level just under the cloud base — appearing and disappearing through wisps of cloud.

"Spitfires! They're Spitfires." Shouted someone over the radio.

"My God. They're heading straight for us, why don't they veer off?" exclaimed Frank.

The two formations of aircraft were closing at nearly 600 miles per hour. Conrad reacted quickly and turned slightly to port to avoid the leader of the formation who shot past him about 25 yards away. Clark was flying Wally's wing on that side and the leader of the formation was heading straight for him ...

* * *

W HAT happened in the next minute or two has been described in many books in many ways, almost all of them misleading. It was only in 2005 that the author received a copy of the following report from RAF HQ at Hendon:

"From: O.C. No.421 Squadron

To: Air Ministry, P.4 (CAS)(CAN)
 74-77 Oxford St., London W.1

cc: B.P.S.O. RAF Station,
 Clifton Yorks,
 83 Group (REAR)
 127 Wing HQ

Date: 15 June 1944

Ref: 421S/20/P.1

Circumstantial Report
CAN.J.4924 F/L F.J. Clark Spitfire IX.B. NH415

1. 421 Squadron took off from Landing Strip B.2, four miles N.E. of Bayeux at 1700 hours on the second patrol of the day. This

operation was a patrol of the Assault Area. The squadron was led by the O.C. S/L W.A.G. Conrad.

2. F/L Clark was flying Red 2 position to the C.O.

3. The squadron was flying on a south-westerly course five miles north of Caen at 1730 hours. A formation of Spitfires was seen approaching at the same level at cloud base which was 1200 feet.

4. The O.C. turned slightly to avoid the leader of the other formation and he passed about 25 yards on the starboard side. At that point the leader of the other formation and F/L Clark who was Red 2, both saw that a collision was inevitable. Both banked steeply to starboard and the aircraft met head-on. A wing was torn from F/L Clark's aircraft. It flamed about the cockpit, dove straight down, crashed and blew up.

5. This aircraft was fitted with Merlin 66 engine 162927/A.448274

6. It was later discovered that the other aircraft was piloted by W/C L.V. Chadburn, DSO, DFC and bar. His aircraft disintegrated in the air.

7. RAF Station Tangmere Signal T.794 dated 13.6.44 refers.

(L.G. Hennessey) F/O for O.C. No. 421 Squadron"

Medical staff reported that Chadburn survived the crash, severely wounded and unconscious, but he died before he reached the medical station. He is interred in Rainville Cemetery five miles (8 kilometres) north-east of Caen, Section V, Row R, Grave 2. He was 25. Clark is buried at Bretteville-sur-Laize Cemetery 15 miles (24 kilometres) south of Caen, Section XXIV, Row C, Grave 5.

Chapter Eleven

Dear Joe,

IT'S YOUR SON, Barry. Up until recently I really didn't know who you were. But things have changed dramatically, and the opening chapter of this book describes how. But let me go back and start at the beginning of my emerging consciousness — which unfortunately hadn't quite developed before you left.

My earliest recollection is standing up in my crib looking down through the nursery's upstairs window into the back yard and wanting to get out there and play. I was living with my mother and her parents whom I called Nana and Bubba in a two-storey home on the west side of Hampton Avenue in Montreal. In the winter huge blowers piled snow up in large mountains on the front lawns. This provided terrific opportunities for building caves and forts and build them I did. Years went by and I remember learning how to use a hammer and saw in the basement with my grandfather. But the concept of father or even grandfather was unknown to me. It was Nana and Bubba and Mom — that was life and the family unit as I knew it.

Although at first it seemed like a bit of an adventure when Mom's new friend Bill turned up after we had moved into a lower duplex on the East side of McClynne Avenue, life seemed to be just unfolding. I had no comparable reference as I really didn't know any other families. Things began to change, however, after I attended their wedding. I couldn't manage to get the confetti to shake out of the tightly packed cellophane bag, but when I returned to the apartment after seeing them off to New York on a Trans Canada Airlines DC-3, I discovered my Mom's wedding hat filled with confetti on the coffee table and also a brand new, operational, toy steam shovel to move it all around.

That was August 1948 and then I vaguely remember driving to Belleville where we moved in with Reverend Sparling and his wife in a rambling farmhouse across from Christ Church and I started kindergarten. Somewhere around that time I also remember being teased by some wicked neighborhood kids about being an orphan — I guess Mom had told me something about the fact that I actually had a missing father but now had a new one. In the late Fall when we moved into our brand new brick bungalow in Reynold's Crescent along with a dozen other Northern Electric Company families, it was sort of a difficult transition for everyone. As you had been basically raised by adoring aunts and grandparents in Brampton until your father remarried and then had to cope with the new law and order of a stepmother, I also had a somewhat similar experience. It was sure tough without you, Joe, although it's conceivable that it would have been tough with you as well — in different ways — for I was a handful growing up. There was an independent spirit inside me that never wavered. But my parents have consistently supported me, particularly financially, although clearly, I didn't turn out to be what they had in mind.

Over time I acquired bits and pieces of your life mostly from my Brampton aunts along with a few references from Mom, but you didn't have a personality in my mind — I had no idea what you were like. There were almost no references made to any resemblance I had to you.

Many more years went by and as I got older the status quo became unbearable. This sense of not being disrespectful of my stepfather by getting to know more about my actual father and the always accompanying sense of guilt because I didn't know more, began to give way to an increasing desire to find out who you were. I also began to have an overwhelming need to identify where you were in me — my 'Clarkness'. But the trail seemed to be cold. Both aunts had passed on, all documents and letters to and from you had been let go — perhaps in a new beginning. And the few black and white pictures I had, just showed a person who usually looked happy posing for the camera but exhibited no identifiable persona. Pictures can remind us of someone we knew but if you've never known them, their pictures aren't quite worth a thousand words. I hadn't experienced your life or your death. "Only the forgotten truly die," someone said, "while the remembered live on within us." You have to have known someone before you might forget them and I felt stuck in between — trying to remember a father I hadn't known.

On one occasion I drove up to Brampton and discovered that the house where you initially grew up at 358 Main Street was still there but was surrounded by encroaching new development — no longer the rural setting you had enjoyed as a young boy and later as a young man. The front porch had been cut off to widen the street as far as possible, and the rest of the structure had been painted pink. It's now a fabric store.

Fate placed me in that house temporarily as well, during another transitional period for me — in between flunking out of Engineering but electing to go back into Arts. That day forty years later, I felt overwhelmed with regret that I hadn't used my five months there with Aunt Doris to collect every shred of information about you that I could. Instead of feeling guilty, at that time, about finding a letter from you in the attic describing how June was different in your heart from the others — I should have been stuffing my pockets with everything that spoke of you. I guess I was too preoccupied with myself then. The timing was wrong at least.

And there I found myself sitting in the car in an empty parking lot across the street staring at the window of the bedroom we were both familiar with. It was a bright, freezing February afternoon and I wanted to break in to see if there was anything left under the eaves. I was overcome with anguish. It was a turning point — it became a clear focus to find out more but I didn't know how it could be achieved at that late date.

Aunt Helen had given me an old album that had been put together by your Grandpa Herbert in memory of Florence your Mom. I had looked through it but didn't recognize anyone. I decided to examine it much more carefully — finding information on the back of some pictures by peeling and steaming off the glue. I decided to go back to Brampton to try to find her grave-site.

On another chilly afternoon a friend and I drove into the main cemetery, parked the car, and began to search all around. One of the album pictures showed a tall distinctive monument but we weren't having any luck until an elderly gentleman appeared out of nowhere riding a bike and asked us if he could help. "I'm looking for Florence Clark and Herbert's site," I said. "Oh it's right over there beside your car," he replied! Then he virtually seemed to disappear from view. We had come full circle and there it was! The family plot included a small marker for a brother of yours you never knew as he had died as a baby. There was also a recent inscription on the main stone acknowledging that you were buried at Bretteville-sur-Laize. I felt ashamed that I didn't even know where that was although I had faded pictures of your original white wooden cross and of the stone that replaced it.

When I got hooked up to the internet I immediately entered your 'name' in a search and found a number of people around the world using it. And trying to find you in the Department of Veteran's Affairs site was unsuccessful. Fleeting thoughts that maybe you were still alive gave way to more rationally sending an e-mail to DVA asking why there was no record of you. Their response was that the person responsible for the information was away and that they would get back to me. Months went by but suddenly they replied giving me the address to find your page. I went there and then immediately did a search with the new information — "June 13, 1944" and "421 Squadron". (The reader could do the same with the same results!) The first URL delivered a clear photograph of you and the story of your death under the heading "The Blackest Day in 421 Squadron History". I was absolutely stunned — I poured through the entire site, that around 14,000 people had already been to, and got to where you could leave a message for the site administrator D Clark — not at all thinking that the name Clark had any significance beyond coincidence.

Within an hour Uncle Dave appeared on my screen! It wasn't as if you had just walked in the door but it was surely the next best thing! Little did I know that there was so much more going to happen.

For weeks we exchanged detailed e-mails about our lives, shared scraps of information and gradually a new version of you began to take shape. It wasn't very complete but compared to what little I had — it was very beneficial. Dave had spent the last several years researching everything he could find about you, mostly in official documents, and sent me an unpublished biography of you he had written for the family. He also had genealogical information dating back to 1756! We had the first of many pub lunches — all mostly focused on the war and you. More pictures surfaced through the internet from the daughter of one of your colleagues — they were candid and showed you as an admired leader, charismatic, and an instigator who enjoyed a good prank.[†] These shots spoke volumes at the time, although it was really all we had. But it was progress.

When I read the biography of W/C Lloyd Vernon Chadburn, DSO and bar, DFC entitled *Gone is the Angel,* written by Robert W Forbes[‡], I thought it might be informative, in some way, to contact his son. Looking for an address I reached the author only to learn that Andrew had just died two weeks earlier. This was more incentive for us to press on. And when Dave offered to take me over to Tangmere and Bretteville-sur-Laize for the 60th anniversary of D-Day celebrations I was stunned again. I wondered how I would cope with it all emotionally and what I would potentially learn.

The museum at Tangmere does a good job in providing a glimpse of life as it was while you were there but we both wanted more than that. The runways are overgrown and a huge hydroponics pepper greenhouse has replaced the hangars. And just one Spitfire — frozen in time — but now on the cover of this book!

There were many crowded ceremonies at various locations and cemeteries in Normandy and we elected to visit your grave on the same day an event was scheduled there. Arriving quite early in the morning, the sun was low in the sky casting long dark shadows from each of the 2,872 head stones. But even then, we discovered there were already busy preparations being made. Mounties in cheerful, bright red uniforms, school children arriving from buses with flowers and flags, banner-carrying representatives from each of the communities liberated after D-Day were all milling around. Canada's Governor General chatted with veterans and exuberant bands began playing wonderful anthems — all in conjunction with the actual ceremony.

---

† see: http://www3.sympatico.ca/angels_eight/clark02.html
‡ Brown Books, Toronto 1997, ISBN 0-9681875-0-1

I knew the general area where the marker was but decided to just read inscriptions, row upon row, until I naturally arrived at yours. I was struck, of course, by the ages of those honoured. Twenty-one, eighteen, twenty-two, nineteen and then you at twenty-three. I dropped to my knees. My whole system froze in one long deep sigh — I was, at last, there. I still don't have the words to describe how I felt — there probably aren't any.

We spent most of the day in the cemetery. The place was filled with so much sunshine, life, and pageantry — probably more than there ever had been before and perhaps more than there ever will be again — at least in our lifetimes. It was absolutely the best day, in all the days of my life, to be in that spot. It seemed like a loop had been closed and I could go home — somehow more complete. But Dave's magic wasn't finished.

A few months after our return and during a time when I was in a state of not expecting any further knowledge about you — your old pal Bev, who unknown to me was alive and well in the Eastern Townships in Quebec, picked up Dave's book *Angels Eight — Normandy Air War Diary,* and contacted him. He said he had kept all of your 50 letters and would send them to us along with some pictures.

Reading your letters, mostly in the order they were written, was a thorough, spellbinding experience. You sounded so familiar to me — and why not? Through a whole afternoon of reading — you did go on at length — I felt strangely comfortable. Finally it was becoming crystal clear who you were and why I am ... quite similar. It was comforting and personally validating to realize that we would have been good buddies and would have shared compatible personalities. It was a very personal glimpse of you that was heaven sent by a Godfather.

And how did a popular party guy, an English major, a theatre person and an independent spirit sign up to fly planes and wage war against the forces of evil overseas? Where did this come from? What was your real motivation? You had finished high school and needed a job? There apparently wasn't money or support available for you to go to university although, according to Bev, everyone thought that should have been a natural thing for you to do.

Well, one of your earliest letters which I now have was probably written in that Main Street room we shared at different times. You needed to gain weight in order to be accepted into the Air Force and what better way to do so than a vacation with the grandparents and aunts. In a letter to Bev dated 5 July 1940, at the age of nineteen in Brampton, you wrote about appreciating the total support in the community for the war effort:

My grandmother is not at all keen on my entering the Air Force, but everyone else is quite pleased. You know Joe, I really think that up here, among these people, I have found something that not only accounts for my desire to join up but has given me a certain feeling that I have never quite experienced before. I am quite certain that if and when I am sworn in to the Air Force, it will be no hypocrite that pledges allegiance to his King

Questions answered! At nineteen, when I was sitting in that room, I was concerned with trying to learn how to play the five-string banjo!

The early letters give me a very intimate vision of your life as a man, a trainee and then as an instructor itching to get overseas. You were such a force — keeping in touch with so many friends and relatives and also keeping them in touch with each other. The Joes remained family even after they were spread all over the world in an age when communication was very slow although letters, remarkably, found their way through it all.

Then I read about the engagement, the wedding, the honeymoon in New York and, of course, my birth. I loved the marvelously pastoral letter written on a Saturday afternoon in Aylmer when I'm sleeping and you are listening to various passages of music and weaving reflections into the text about many of the overtures, operatic arias and marches that are wafting around the apartment along with the aromas from your *"fine wife's cooking"*. Some of the descriptions I found to be just so well informed — then I realized that you might just be incorporating some of liner notes on those old 78 albums.

Perhaps I wasn't entirely sleeping though. From when I was around eleven I listened to those same records over and over again down in the basement where they were stored — not knowing that they were your selections and were your favourites.

And here's one of my favourites, a letter from RCAF Station Bagotville after leaving Aylmer and with Mom and I back at her parents:

25 April 1943

He is doing marvelously well, Joe, and I must comment on how lucky we have been both before and after he arrived. He has never been anything but a great big bundle of happiness for Junie and I.

Until I read those words I had no idea what you thought of me and didn't have any sense of what I meant to you. What a treasure those lines provide. And you go on in that letter to talk about another love in your life:

It has been the type of flying I've always wanted to do but never been able to because of the dammed student in the front seat who was the only reason I was in the back seat and therefore for whom I had to fly precisely, accurately and safely in order to install in him the confidence necessary in a pilot. But up here they've been training us to be fighter pilots and the whole flying course revolves on formation flying, dog fighting, and low flying — for all of which I have a very soft spot in my heart. And then of course flying a Hurricane is a thrill and a pleasure in itself. And I think I appreciate everything all the more because I've waited two years to get to it. In any case with the prospects of being in combat within the next three or four months, the world has taken on a wonderful rosy complexion

In many of the letters, Joe, you deliver a complete sense of the total environment you find yourself in — the flavour of the room, the light quality at that time of day, your precise mood with it's accompanying thoughts swirling around. I can feel the ache of your separation from key people and I marvel at the good humour you brought to all those moments. Until now I've always thought of you in black and white. Because of your brother Dave's relentless research and his books which brought Bev back into our lives with the letters — you have become a person with colours for the first time in my awareness. The day I first became aware of Dave I phoned my friend Jennifer Cline and blurted out. "I have an Uncle — I have an identity!!" She has followed the story from the visit to Brampton cemetery and was prompted and inspired to provide us with a revised, fresh, new portrait — an image of a person not in black and white and featured on the cover.

In one letter you make a reference to writing a book. All my life I've wanted to write a book or a feature film script but continually realized I didn't know what I wanted to say. It's so ironic that it is because of you, and about you, that I end up at least participating in a book. I'm an old man looking at you almost as if you are a young, but extremely accomplished son who is growing up in the letters through four tumultuous years in our history, a son who didn't get the chance to grow up any further but now can still inspire me!

Here's a portion of what Bev wrote in a letter that didn't get there in time, dated 25 June 1944:

Let us go back to college Frankie!!! We need the instruction and it will, at the very least, give us a breathing spell in which to look around and view the situation. We could live together in some small place — like les bohemians of Paris — with our wives.

What can I say? It certainly strikes a chord with me. I suspect that I could have done that easily. It turns out that my life has progressed very much in that general direction even in the absence of both of you.

After knowing so little, I now feel so much more about you and have a new family friend and Uncle. Although I've read all the letters — I'm still rereading them. Here and there, and in random order, I'll appreciate a turn of phrase or an idea or gain an impression of you that seems to have become even more real. As the process of knowing you continues, even at my age, it inspires me to be a little bolder with my life and my Clarkness. And, of course, Dave and I continue to compare notes every once in a while at the Pub. A pint, a Pub Club, another pint and then a coffee; we don't even have to order. But when this book comes out we may move into a different phase — the waitress will probably notice that we look different and will bring us a fresh menu to embark on.

While I'm privileged to have the last words in this book, Joe, I'd like to quote the only words I had from you until your letters surfaced. In a small book of poetry which was yours, and probably was beside you at Tangmere, you have bracketed these lines from Alfred, Lord Tennyson's *Crossing the Bar* and have written: *Must show this to Bev !*

It seems like an appropriate way to close this chapter. Respectfully,

your son,

Barry

Twilight and evening bell,
And after that the dark!
And may there be no sadness or farewell,
When I embark;
For tho' from out our bourne of Time and Place
The flood may bear me far,
I hope to see my Pilot face to face
When I have crost the bar.

Appendix A — Pilots in 421 Squadron

Abbreviations used in the tables:

109 — Me 109 German fighter
110 — Me 110 German fighter
190 — FW 190 German fighter
88 — Ju 88 German bomber
AA — hit by anti-aircraft fire
AFC — "A" Flight commander
b/o — baled out
BFC — "B" Flight commander
c/l — crash landed
coll — collision
dam — claimed a damaged enemy aircraft
dest — claimed a destroyed enemy aircraft
EOT — end of tour
EVD — evaded capture after parachuting to earth
F/L — Flight Lieutenant
F/O — Flying Officer
F/S — Flight Sergeant
FTR — failed to return from a mission
GF — shot down by German fighter
hosp — hospitalized
KIA — killed in action
MF — mechanical failure
n/e — non effective, ruled unfit to fly by a medical board
P/O — Pilot Officer
POW — prisoner of war
pro — promoted
prob — claimed a probably destroyed enemy aircraft
SC — squadron commander
sh — shared claim of a destroyed enemy aircraft
S/L — Squadron Leader
Sq — squadron
st — started with the squadron
W/C — Wing Commander
WO2 — Warrant Officer 2nd Class

October 1943

S/L R W 'Buck' McNair	SC		190 1 Oct, pro W/C 16 Oct
	SC	S/L C M 'Chuck' Magwood	st 16 Oct, dam 190 24 Oct
F/O J N 'Jack' Bamford			pro F/O 25 Oct
P/O W M 'Bill' Barnett			c/l 18 Oct
P/O A C 'Brandy' Brandon			
F/L R A 'Bob' Buckham			to 403 pro S/L 5 Oct
		F/L F J 'Frank' Clark	st 30 Oct
F/O W F 'Cookie' Cook			pro F/O 1 Oct, sh 190 3 Oct, FTR 3 Oct
		P/O J F 'Jimmy' Davidson	st 7 Oct, pro F/O 25 Oct
P/O T J 'Tommy' DeCourcy			
P/O N B Dixon			
F/O R G 'Gord' Driver			dam 190 24 Oct
F/O W 'Johnny' Drope			
F/L A E Fleming	BFC		BFC 4 Oct, sick 18 Oct
F/O i R 'Ian' Forster			FTR 22 Oct
S/L F E 'Freddie' Green			to 416 Sq 23 Oct, cold 18 Oct
		F/O R J 'Bob' Grigg	st 29 Oct
F/L W E 'Web' Harten	AFC		
P/O J S Hicks			190 3 Oct
F/O R W Isbister			pro F/O 2 Oct
F/L P 'Paul' Johnson			dam 190 22 Oct
F/O K H 'Karl' Linton			sh 190 3 Oct, 190 18 Oct, 190 22 Oct
F/O A R 'Andy' MacKenzie			190 22 Oct
F/L R D Phillip	BFC		EOT 4 Oct
F/O P A 'Percy' McLachlan			pro F/O 2 Oct, sick 18 Oct
		F/O H C 'Scotty' McRoberts	st 30 Oct
F/O P C Musgrave			
F/O R A 'Ralph' Nickerson			
F/O J A 'Red' Omand			
P/O H R Packard			190 3 Oct
P/O T 'Tommy' Parks			
F/L J N 'John' Paterson			
F/L W 'Wally' Quint			
		F/L G D 'Robbie' Robertson	st 23 Oct
F/L F J 'Johnny' Sherlock			
F/L L R 'Len' Thorne			
F/O T S Todd			
F/O W 'Willie' Warfield			
F/O D K Wilson			to HQ 17 Oct
F/L H P 'Hank' Zary			

November 1943

S/L C M 'Chuck' Magwood	SC		190 3 Nov
F/O J N 'Jack' Bamford			
P/O W M Barnett			
P/O A C 'Brandy' Brandon			pro F/O 19 Nov
F/L F J 'Frank' Clark			sick 28 Nov
P/O J F 'Jimmy' Davidson			
P/O T J 'Tommy' DeCourcy			
P/O N B Dixon			
F/O R G 'Gord' Driver			
F/O W 'Johnny' Drope			
F/L A E Fleming	BFC		prob 109 3 Nov
F/O R J 'Bob' Grigg			broken leg b/o 23 Nov
F/L W E 'Web' Harten	AFC		
F/O J S Hicks			pro F/O 19 Nov
F/O R W Isbister			
F/L P 'Paul' Johnson			
F/O K H 'Karl' Linton			
F/O A R 'Andy' MacKenzie			
F/O P A 'Percy' McLachlan			back 2 Nov
F/O H C 'Scotty' McRoberts			
F/O P C Musgrave			pro F/L 17 Nov, sick 20 Nov
F/O R A 'Ralph' Nickerson			
F/O J A "Red" Omand			
P/O H R Packard			
P/O T 'Tommy' Parks			
F/L J N 'John' Paterson			
F/L W 'Wally' Quint			
F/L G D 'Robbie' Robertson			
F/L F J 'Johnny' Sherlock			dam 109 3 Nov
F/L L R 'Len' Thorne			
F/O T S Todd			EOT 21 Nov
F/O W 'Willie' Warfield			
		F/L R C 'Roger' Wilson	st ??
F/L H P 'Hank' Zary			

December 1943

Name	Unit	Name	Notes
S/L C M 'Chuck' Magwood	SC		to HQ 13 Dec, sick 3 Dec
		S/L J F 'Jimmy' Lambert	st 13 Dec, 190 20 Dec KIA 20 Dec
F/O J N 'Jack' Bamford			
P/O W M Barnett			to 402 31 Dec
P/O A C 'Brandy' Brandon			hosp n/e 28 Dec
F/L F J 'Frank' Clark			back 1 Dec, sick 12 Dec
P/O J F 'Jimmy' Davidson			back 1 Dec
P/O T J 'Tommy' DeCourcy			
P/O N B Dixon			to 416 31 Dec
F/O R G 'Gord' Driver			
F/O W 'Johnny' Drope			
F/L A E Fleming	BFC		sick 3 Dec EOT 14 Dec
	BFC	F/L E L 'Ed' Gimbel	st BFC 14 Dec, 190 20 Dec
F/O R J 'Bob' Grigg			
F/L W E 'Web' Harten	AFC		EOT 14 Dec
		F/O R 'Dick' Henry	st 29 Dec
F/O J S Hicks			
F/O R W Isbister			
F/L P 'Paul' Johnson			hosp 8 Dec, n/e 15 Dec
F/O K H 'Karl' Linton	AFC		back 6 Dec, 190 20 Dec, pro F/L AFC 14 Dec
F/O A R 'Andy' MacKenzie			(2) 190, 109 20 Dec
F/O P A 'Percy' McLachlan			
F/O H C 'Scotty' McRoberts			
		F/O R 'Bob' Murray	st 29 Dec
F/O P C Musgrave			
F/O R A 'Ralph' Nickerson			
F/O J A 'Red' Omand			
F/O H R Packard			pro F/O
P/O T 'Tommy' Parks			
F/L J N 'John' Paterson			hosp 11 Dec
F/L W 'Wally' Quint			sick 3 Dec
F/L G D 'Robbie' Robertson			
F/L F J 'Johnny' Sherlock			
F/L L R 'Len' Thorne			
F/O W 'Willie' Warfield			hosp 7 Dec, pro P/O 13 Dec, sick 21 Dec
F/L R C 'Roger' Wilson			hosp 11 Dec, cycle accident 28 Dec
F/L H P 'Hank' Zary			c/l 21 Dec

January 1944

		S/L W A G 'Wally' Conrad	st 1 Jan
F/O J N 'Jack' Bamford			
P/O A C 'Brandy' Brandon			n/e 4 Jan
		P/O J A Brown	st 12 Jan
F/L F J 'Frank' Clark			
		F/O L F 'Lorne' Curry	st 12 Jan
P/O J F 'Jimmy' Davidson			
P/O T J 'Tommy' DeCourcy			AA 3 Jan
F/O R G 'Gord' Driver			
F/L W 'Johnny' Drope			pro F/L
F/L E L 'Ed' Gimbel	BFC		
		F/L C D 'Bitsy' Grant	st 12 Jan
F/O R J 'Bob' Grigg			
F/O R W 'Dick' Henry			
F/O J S Hicks			
F/O R W Isbister			EOT 4 Jan
F/L P 'Paul' Johnson			
F/O K H 'Karl' Linton	AFC		AA 3 Jan
F/O A R 'Andy' MacKenzie			DFC 17 Jan
		F/L J F 'Johnny' McElroy	st 5 Jan
F/O P A 'Percy' McLachlan			c/l 23 Jan
F/O H C 'Scotty' McRoberts			hosp 17 Jan
F/O R 'Bob' Murray			
F/O P C Musgrave			
F/O R A 'Ralph' Nickerson			
		F/O H H 'Pat' O'Hair	st 5 Jan, left 14 Jan
F/O J A 'Red' Omand			EOT 4 Jan
F/O H R Packard			
P/O T 'Tommy' Parks			EOT 4 Jan
F/L J N 'John' Paterson			
F/L W 'Wally' Quint			
F/L G D 'Robbie' Robertson			
F/L F J 'Johnny' Sherlock			
F/L L R 'Len' Thorne			
F/O W 'Willie' Warfield			
F/L R C 'Roger' Wilson			n/e 4 Jan, back 25 Jan
F/L H P 'Hank' Zary			hosp 10 Jan

February 1944

S/L W A G 'Wally Conrad			sick 9 Feb
F/O J N 'Jack' Bamford			
P/O A C 'Brandy' Brandon			back 2 Feb
P/O J A Brown			
F/L F J 'Frank' Clark			
F/O L F 'Lorne' Curry			
P/O J F 'Jimmy' Davidson			
P/O T J 'Tommy' DeCourcy			EOT 29 Feb
F/O R G 'Gord' Driver			
F/L W 'Johnny' Drope			
F/L E L 'Ed' Gimbel	BFC		
F/L C D 'Bitsy' Grant			
F/O R J 'Bob' Grigg			
F/O R W 'Dick' Henry			
F/O J S Hicks			EOT 29 Feb
F/L P 'Paul' Johnson			
F/O K H 'Karl' Linton	AFC		
F/O A R 'Andy' MacKenzie			
F/L J F 'Johnny' McElroy			
F/O P A 'Percy' McLachlan			hosp 21 Feb, out 26 Feb
F/O H C 'Scotty' McRoberts			
F/O R 'Bob' Murray			hosp 21 Feb, out 26 Feb
F/O P C Musgrave			
F/O R A 'Ralph' Nickerson			
F/O H R Packard			EOT 29 Feb
F/L J N 'John' Paterson			
F/L W 'Wally' Quint			
F/L G D 'Robbie' Robertson			month in Canada 10 Feb
F/L F J 'Johnny' Sherlock			EOT 29 Feb
F/L L R 'Len' Thorne			
F/O W 'Willie' Warfield			
		P/O W D Wendt	st 13 Feb
F/L R C 'Roger' Wilson			back 15 Feb
F/L H P 'Hank' Zary			sick 21 Feb, out 26 Feb

March 1944

S/L W A G 'Wally' Conrad			course 14 Mar
F/O J N 'Jack' Bamford			
P/O A C 'Brandy' Brandon			
P/O J A Brown			
F/L F J 'Frank' Clark			
F/O L F 'Lorne' Curry			
P/O J F 'Jimmy' Davidson			
F/O R G 'Gord' Driver			
F/L W 'Johnny' Drope			c/l 2 Mar, shot huts 5 Mar
		F/O B T 'Benton' Gilmour	st 22 Mar
F/L E L 'Ed' Gimbel	BFC		acting SC 14 Mar
F/L C D 'Bitsy' Grant			c/l 3 Mar
F/O R J 'Bob' Grigg			
F/O R W 'Dick' Henry			hosp 9 Mar
F/L P 'Paul' Johnson			
F/O K H 'Karl' Linton	AFC		c/l 9 Mar
F/O A R 'Andy' MacKenzie			married 25 Mar
		F/O McCurdy	st 19 Mar
F/L J F 'Johnny' McElroy			
F/O P A 'Percy' McLachlan			left ? Mar
F/O H C 'Scotty' McRoberts			
F/O R 'Bob' Murray			
F/O P C Musgrave			hosp 9 Mar
F/O R A 'Ralph' Nickerson			
F/L J N 'John' Paterson			
F/L W 'Wally' Quint			to HQ 28 Mar
		F/O G M 'Gordie' Smith	hosp 9 Mar
		F/L W N 'Bill' Stronach	st 5 Mar, pro F/L 27 Mar
F/L L R 'Len' Thorne			
F/O W 'Willie' Warfield			shot huts 5 Mar
P/O W D Wendt			left ? Mar
F/L R C 'Roger' Wilson			hosp 9 Mar
F/L H P 'Hank' Zary			hosp 9 Mar

April 1944

S/L W A G 'Wally' Conrad			back from course 7 Apr
F/O J N 'Jack' Bamford			
P/O A C 'Brandy' Brandon			
P/O J A Brown			to HQ 1 Apr
F/L F J 'Frank' Clark			
F/O L F 'Lorne' Curry			
P/O J F 'Jimmy' Davidson			
F/O R G 'Gord' Driver			
F/L W 'Johnny' Drope			
F/O B T 'Benton' Gilmour			
F/L E L 'Ed' Gimbel	BFC		big party for Godefroy 29 Apr
F/L C D 'Bitsy' Grant			
F/O R J 'Bob' Grigg			
F/O R W 'Dick' Henry			
F/L P 'Paul' Johnson			
F/O K H 'Karl' Linton	AFC		EOT 5 Apr
F/O A R 'Andy' MacKenzie			
F/O McCurdy			st ? Mar, left ? Mar
F/L J F 'Johnny' McElroy			
F/O H C 'Scotty' McRoberts			hit in coup top 11 Apr
F/O R 'Bob' Murray			
F/O R A 'Ralph' Nickerson			pro F/L 26 Apr
F/L J N 'John' Paterson			
	AFC	F/L G D 'Robbie' Robertson	back 4 Apr, AFC 5 Apr
F/O G M 'Gordie' Smith			
F/L W N 'Bill' Stronach			shot at big party 29 Apr
F/L L R 'Len' Thorne			
F/O W 'Willie' Warfield			
F/L R C 'Roger' Wilson			
F/L H P 'Hank' Zary			

May 1944

S/L W A G 'Wally Conrad			teeth fixed 8 May to 12 May
F/O J N 'Jack' Bamford			
P/O A C 'Brandy' Brandon			
		F/O J 'Jack' Calvert	st 24 May
F/L F J 'Frank' Clark			dam 88 8 May
F/O L F 'Lorne' Curry			
P/O J F 'Jimmy' Davidson			AA, b/o, 21 May POW
F/O R G 'Gord' Driver			
F/L W 'Johnny' Drope			
F/O B T 'Benton' Gilmour			
F/O E L 'Ed' Gimbel			
F/L C D 'Bitsy' Grant			
F/O R J 'Bob' Grigg			
F/O R W 'Dick' Henry			AA, b/o, 9 May POW
F/L P 'Paul' Johnson	AFC		AFC 20 May dummies 6 May, 110 and 88 8 May
		F/O LeBlond	st 24 May
F/O A R 'Andy' MacKenzie			To 403 18 May dummies 6 May
F/L J F 'Johnny' McElroy	BFC		BFC 4 May
F/O H C 'Scotty' McRoberts			
F/O R 'Bob' Murray			
F/O R A 'Ralph' Nickerson			AA, b/o, 21 May EVD
F/L J N 'John' Paterson			back after wedding 23 May
F/L G D 'Robbie' Robertson	AFC		Pro S/L 411 20 May
		F/S W 'Bill' Saunders	st25 May
		WO2 Smith	st 24 May left 31 May
F/O G M 'Gordie' Smith			
F/L W N 'Bill' Stronach			back on duty 20 May
		F/S J H 'John' Tetroe	st 25 May
F/L L R 'Len' Thorne			
F/O W 'Willie' Warfield			
F/L R C 'Roger' Wilson			marriage leave 18 May
F/L H P 'Hank' Zary			dam 88 8 May

177

June 1944

S/L W A 'Wally' Conrad	SC		
F/O J N 'Jack' Bamford			3-190 dest 15 June, AA POW 27June, DFC 11 July
F/O A C 'Brandy' Brandon			190 dam 23 June, 190 dam 28 June
		F/O G A 'George' Cashion	st 26 June
F/O J 'Jack' Calvert			
F/L F J 'Frank' Clark			KIA 13 June coll with Chadburn
F/O W F 'Cookie' Cook			190 dest 15 June
F/O L F 'Lorne' Curry			GF in dogfight KIA 15 June
F/O R G 'Gord' Driver			2-109 dam 23 Jun, coll 25 June
F/L W 'Johnny' Drope			MF, b/o over Utah KIA 7 Jun
		F/O J M Flood	st 14 June, AA 17 June safe, 190 dam 28 June
F/L B T 'Benton' Gilmour			GF c/l 15 June
F/O E L 'Ed' Gimbel			to USAAF 4 June
F/L C D 'Bitsy' Grant			coll with Driver KIA 25 June
F/O R J 'Bob' Grigg			MF KIA 7 June lost in Channel
		F/O J Hamm	st 9 June
F/L P G 'Paul' Johnson	AFC		AA 10 June safe, 190 dest 23 June, 3-190 dest 190 dam 30 June
F/O H Leblond			
		P/O E H Levere	st 26 June
		F/O O E Libby	st 27 June
		F/O G L Mayson	st 9 June,190 dest 23 June, n/e
F/L J F 'Johnny' McElroy	BFC		109 dest 15 June, c/l 15 June, 190 dest 23 June, 109 dest 28 June, to S/L 416 29 June,
F/O H C 'Scotty' McRoberts			190 dam 23 Jun, AA 26 June, AA 28 June, 109 dest 30 June
F/O R W 'Bob' Murray			MF KIA 13 June in Channel
F/L J N 'John' Paterson			2-190 dest 15 June
		F/O R W Perkins	st 27 June
F/S W 'Bill' Saunders			to 416 2 June
		F/L E S Smith	st 15 June
F/O G M 'Gordie' Smith			
		F/L G E Stephenson	st 26 June
F/O W N 'Bill' Stronach			2-190 dest 15 June
P/O J H 'John' Tetroe			c/l 10 June, n/e 16 June
F/L L R 'Len' Thorne			
		F/O J Ulmer	st 27 June
		F/S R G Wallace	st 6 June, GF KIA 23 June
F/O W 'Willie' Warfield			2-190 dest 15 June
F/L R C 'Roger' Wilson			190 dest 23 June, 109 dest 30 June
F/L H P 'Hank' Zary	BFC		109 dest 28 June, BFC 29 June

Index

Brown W/C Mannifrank 103, 127, 130, 140, 151
Bryan F/O Tommy 118
Buckham S/L Bob 102

C

Caen vi, 74, 104, 150, 156, 157, 158
Calvert F/O Jack **122,** 177, 178
Cambrai 60, 69, 82, 108
Campbell F/O Black 128
Chadburn Thomas Alonzo 11
Chadburn W/C Lloyd Vernon 5, 8, 22, 101, 102, 103, 123, 126, 128, 130, 136, 139, 141, 142, 143, 155, 163
Churchill Prime Minister Winston 21, 105, 142
Clark Barry Joel iii, iv, 7, 9, 10, 12, 29, **31,** 38, 81, 159, 168
Clark David 5, 9, 10, 162, 166
Clark Frank Allen 11, 26
Clark June (Hart) 28, 29, 30, **31,** 32, 38, 41, 45
Cline Jennifer iv, 167
Cockshott Andrew 6, 7, 8, 9
Communism 17
Conrad S/L Wally 63, **71,** 72, 82, 87, 101, 102, 103, 115, 121, **122,** 127, 132, 134, 148, 151, 158, 174, 175, 176, 177
Cook F/O Bill 53, **98, 122**
Curry F/O Lorne **122,** 127
Cuthbertson F/O 'Cuthy' 128

D

D-Day 3, 5, 10, 11, 99, 119, 120, 121, 123, 127, 128, 132, 136, 137, 154, 163
Dakota DC-3 transport 152, **153**
Davidson F/O Jimmy 118
DeCourcy F/O Tommy 57, 62
Dennison F/O Richard 96

De Havilland Tiger Moth 24, 26, 27, 44, 65
DFC vii, 4, 54, 55, 62, 63, 67, 71, 101, 104, 128, 139, 158, 163, 173, 178
Dieppe vi, 72, 116
Dive-bombing method 91
Doris. *See* Aunt Doris
Driver F/O Gordie **122,** 127, 151
Drope F/L Johnny **99,** 121, **122,** 123, 148
DSO 4, 101, 129, 139, 158, 163
Dunkirk vi, 19, 20, 21, 33, 59

E

Eastern Townships 3, 5, 164
East Grinstead Burn Centre 149
Edinburgh 34, 35, 36, 41, 43, 46
EFTS vii, 22, 23, 24

F

Fascism 17
Finley F/L Hart 104
Fisher S/L 154
Flak 46, 59, 72, 74, 75, 78, 79, 92, 96, 107, 108, 112, 115, 116, 118, 119, 120, 123, 125, 137, 147, 148, 150, 156
Fleet Finch 24, 27
Fleming F/L Al 54, 55, 61
Flying Fortress US 8th AF B-17 bomber 73, 78
Forbes-Roberts F/L Dick 128
Forecast D-Day casualties 83, 120
For Whom the Bell Tolls 88
FW 190 German fighter vii, 54, 57, 60, 62, 63, 67, 77, 79, 80, 107, 116, 118, 169

G

Galland Alfred famous German ace 60
Gilmour F/L Benton 116, **122**

4, 146,

178

Printed in the United States
46582LVS00003B/22-138

9 781425 900274